VOCABULARY

for Christian Schools™
Second Edition

Teacher's Edition

Edith E. Smith

BJU PRESS

GREENVILLE, SOUTH CAROLINA

PHOTO CREDITS:
The following agencies and individuals have furnished materials to meet the photographic needs of this textbook. We wish to express our gratitude to them for their important contribution.

Chapter 2
COREL Corporation 4

Chapter 5
PhotoDisc/Getty Images 10

Chapter 12
PhotoDisc/Getty Images 24

Chapter 15
PhotoDisc/Getty Images 30

NOTE:
The fact that materials produced by other publishers are referred to in this volume does not constitute an endorsement by BJU Press of the content or theological position of materials produced by such publishers. The position of BJU Press, and of Bob Jones University, is well known. Any references and ancillary materials are listed as an aid to the student or the teacher and in an attempt to maintain the accepted academic standards of the publishing industry.

VOCABULARY for Christian Schools™: Level D Teachers's Edition
Second Edition

Edith E. Smith, M.A.

Consultants
Candy Cates
Elizabeth Rose, M.Ed., M.A.

Project Editors
Elizabeth A. McAchren
Rebecca A. Osborne

Designer
Nathan Kirsop

Cover Design
John Bjerk
Elly Kalagayan

Composition
Agnieszka Augustyniak
Beata Augustyniak

Project Manager
Denijer Peña

Photo Acquisition
Carla Thomas

Illustrators
Matt Bjerk
Dave Schuppert

Produced in cooperation with the Bob Jones University School of Education and Bob Jones Academy.

for Christian Schools is a registered trademark of BJU Press.

ISBN 1-59166-183-8

15 14 13 12 11 10 9 8 7 6 5 4 3 2

Vocabulary Series
Second Edition Introduction

Since its introduction in the 1980s, the BJU Press *VOCABULARY for Christian Schools* has helped thousands of students increase their vocabulary skills. The philosophy behind the series is a reflection of the BJU Press philosophy as a whole: We use scripturally sound principles that enable teachers to give students the tools to truly comprehend the material at hand.

Thus you will not find in these texts long lists of words to memorize. Rather, the emphasis of the series is on vocabulary principles, such as where our language came from; what common prefixes, roots, and suffixes mean; and how to discern the meaning of a new word based on already understood concepts.

VOCABULARY for Christian Schools may also double as a spelling text. Required words are listed in the Contents; words taught incidentally can be added to the list. Please see "To the Teacher" for further information on many other features of the books and how to best implement the series in your Christian school or home school.

It is our desire that students come away from the texts with a greater understanding of and love for the English language, a gift from the Lord, who is the Giver of all good things.

"How forcible are right words!"
—Job 6:25

Contents

To the Teacher

This vocabulary series, a part of the English curriculum, can strengthen students' reading and writing skills.

Rationale

- Primary emphasis is word contexts of various kinds as the means of learning word meanings. Contexts are primarily from the Bible and from subjects generally taught at the grade level of each vocabulary text.

- Etymology is emphasized: Latin and Greek word parts, native English words, and words from several other languages.

Sequential Plan of the Series

- Levels A–C (grades 7–9): Latin prefixes, roots, suffixes

- Level D (grade 10): Greek combining forms

- Levels A–D: spelling principles, synonyms, antonyms, homonyms, word families, clipped words, blends, compounds, onomatopoetic words

- Level E (grade 11): some of the ways we acquire words—such as allusions, coining, back-formation, folk etymology, borrowing from other languages

- Level F (grade 12): some ways word meanings change, more words borrowed from other languages, native English words

- Levels A and B are interchangeable; likewise levels E and F are interchangeable. Levels C and D are better not interchanged.

Optional Plans for the Series in the English Curriculum

- Cover each book in a semester.
  Half a lesson twice a week (15 to 20 minutes each) or a whole lesson once a week (20 to 30 minutes). (Nearly all lessons are two-part.)

- Cover each book in two semesters.
  Half a lesson twice a week, every other week to allow ample time for Challengers, word stories, cumulative reviews, activities suggested in the supplement, and possible expansion of the lessons.

- Use the books as spelling texts. (Required words are listed in the Contents. Words taught incidentally can be added to the list.)

Features of the Series

- Each book stands alone: the series can be begun at any level.

- Each lesson is two pages.

- Presentation methods are varied.
  Principle, illustration, practice
  Context clues of word meanings, followed by use of the words in other contexts
  Building words from word parts
  Frequent inductive learning
  Seeing how suffixes can determine part of speech
  Going from etymological meaning to present meaning

- Word stories give the origin of words such as *serendipity* and *fantastic* (not intended to be tested).

- Some lessons have Challengers, which are brief, a bit more difficult, and not intended to be tested.

- The *Contents* page includes all the required words and word parts.

- *Cumulative Reviews* emphasize "learning for keeps."

- The *Supplement* includes puzzles, games, contests, and other means of reinforcement and motivation.
  Many items can be adapted to other grade levels.

- The *Reference List* for levels B through F includes word parts previously taught in the series.

- The *Index* contains all words dealt with (required or presented incidentally), word parts, and concepts.

Suggestions for Lesson Presentations

- Begin the book and each lesson with oral reading of the introduction.

- Emphasize "learning for keeps," not just filling in blanks.

- Have students read entire sentence sequences or paragraphs to discover word meanings from context before filling in any blanks.

- Have each student increase his own vocabulary by keeping a notebook of: (1) words from word parts, (2) other contexts of words in the lessons, (3) new words not found in the lessons (meanings discovered from methods taught or from a dictionary), and (4) word families.

- Coordinate with *Writing and Grammar* series and with other studies (e.g., coordination in level F with English literature by citing native English words).

References consulted include *The American Heritage Dictionary, Webster's New World Dictionary, Webster's New Collegiate Dictionary, The American College Dictionary,* and *The Oxford English Dictionary.*

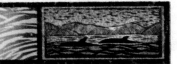

One

A Zest for Words

We can have a humdrum vocabulary or an ever-increasing repertoire of words. Instead of repetitiously saying that we like or love something, we might say, more specifically, that we *relish, delight in, feast on, are fascinated by, revel in, have a proclivity for,* or *have a zest for* something.

Think about some favorite book of yours. Why is it a favorite? It was with words that the author captured your attention. Now think about the reports you write for your classes and the letters you send. Are they interesting because your words are well chosen, making your writing a pleasure to read?

Anything worth saying is worth saying well. You have experiences, thoughts, opinions, and convictions to share. With well-chosen words you can entertain and influence others.

Etymology

To trace a word back to its origin is to study its **etymology.** For example, notice the languages through which we get *etymology:* Middle English, *ethimologie;* Old French and Medieval Latin, *ethimologia;* Latin, *etymologia;* Greek, *etumologia,* from *etumon,* "true, real," and *logy,* "word."

In the transfer of a word from original Greek to modern English, a *u* changes to a *y,* as in *etymology.* Remember this shift in other words of Greek origin.

You can find the Latin word parts from Levels A, B, and C of this series in the Reference List of Word Parts. Ancient Greek is the basis of the **etymological** studies in this book; although the etymologies may contain other languages, only the Greek origins are stressed. In lists of Greek roots, the Greek word endings have been dropped.

Prefixes	***Combining Forms***
epi-/ep-, "on, upon; among"	dem, "people"
poly-, "more than one, many"	graph/gram, "write; something written"
tele-, "distant, far off"	

By separating these English words into their Greek parts, you can find their etymological meanings. Notice that in all of the etymological meanings except the last one the root precedes the prefix.

telegraph, telegram	"write (written) far off"
epigraph, epigram	"write (written) on"
polygraph	"write much"
epidemic	"on or among the people"

To distinguish words with the same etymological meaning—and to know their true meanings today—you need modern definitions.

telegraph	*verb,* "send a message by wire or radio to a receiving station"; *noun,* "a system for sending such messages"
telegram	"a message sent by telegraph"
epigraph	"an inscription engraved on something; a quotation at the beginning of a literary work"
epigram	"a short poem written on a single thought; a concise statement making a point cleverly"
epidemic	"an outbreak and rapid spread of a contagious disease"
polygraph	"an instrument that simultaneously measures breathing, blood pressure, and heartbeat; a lie detector"

From the words in bold type above, choose the right word to complete each sentence, using the definitions to distinguish similar words. You may change the form to plural if necessary.

1. The manager of the drug store uses the _____polygraph_____ to test all applicants for a job. Tim passed the test and was hired to stock the shelves.

2. The regular "stock boy" was one of the first in the community to be affected by the _____epidemic_____ of influenza. Tim would be assigned a different job when the regular boy returned to work.

3. Because Tim's parents were on vacation and not easily reached by telephone, Tim sent them a _____telegram_____ to tell them he had the job.

4. Influenza spreads nearly every winter, the worst winter being 1918–19, when millions died from it, as _____epigraphs_____ on gravestones throughout the world show. This year, though, the flu season was rather short, and the regular stock boy was soon back to work.

Challenger

The Greek *taph* means "tomb." What is another English word for an inscription on a tomb? _____epitaph_____

Combining Forms

We have many compound words, such as *basketball*. Likewise the ancient Greeks often combined words, and we are still combining Greek words. Some Greek words are used so often at the beginning of words that dictionaries call them prefixes; others come at the end of words so often that they are called suffixes. To avoid difficult distinctions, these are listed in the lessons of this book simply as *combining forms*.

Notice the joining of two combining forms to make the English adjective *demographic*. The letter *o* is added to *dem* and to many other Greek roots that have become combining forms.

dem, "people," + *o* + *graph,* "write," + ending -*ic* = demographic

Its related noun, **demographics,** is always plural in form. Both words refer to the study of population—its distribution, growth, size, and so on. Before building a factory or starting a business, planners carefully study the demographics of the locations they have in mind.

Of course, not all words beginning with *dem* or *demo* come from the Greek word for "people." Examples of such unrelated words are *demand, demonstrate, demolish, demon,* and *demote.*

From the following Greek combining forms, make at least five English words.

| photo, "light" | cardio, "heart" | graph/graphy, "write" |
| bio, "life" | ge, "earth" | logy, "science, study" |

photograph, photography, biography, biology, cardiograph, cardiology, geography,

geology, graph, graphology

*Be thou an example of the believers, in word, in conversation, in charity,
in spirit, in faith, in purity.*

—1 Timothy 4:12

Two

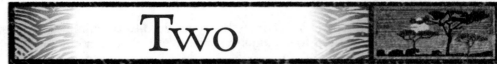

Onomatopoeia

How would you describe the sound of water? You might use the word *trickle, whoosh, splash, ripple, bubble,* or *babble.* These words are made by **onomatopoeia.** Notice the etymology of this word.

> *onomatopoiein,* "coin (make) a name"
>
> *onomat,* "name," + *o* + *poiein,* "make or create"

(As in *demographic,* the letter *o* is added to the first of the two combining forms.)

Spelling the English word with all those vowels is a challenge! Correct pronunciation can help you with most of its eight vowels.

Today the word can mean "the making of a word that imitates the sound it refers to; a word that imitates a sound."

We live in the midst of a multitude of sounds. Descriptive writing can appeal to the sense of sound by using verbs or nouns that imitate sounds. Can you think of other **onomatopoetic** words than those listed above to describe the sound of water? Many onomatopoetic words imitate the sounds of birds and animals: for example, *chirp, woof, purr,* and *whinny.* Some birds, such as the chiff-chaff, get their names from the sounds they make.

Think of the kinds of sounds that you listen to or tune out every day—both pleasing and annoying. Words that imitate these sounds can add vividness to your writing or speaking.

Match the words with what each imitates.

_f_	1. blare	a.	chain
_g_	2. clangor	b.	arrow
_a_	3. clank	c.	bacon frying
_j_	4. clatter	d.	fire in a fireplace
_d_	5. crackle	e.	file on wood or metal
_h_	6. fizz	f.	trumpets
_i_	7. gulp	g.	bell of a fire engine
_e_	8. rasp	h.	carbonated beverage
_c_	9. sizzle	i.	noisy swallowing
_b_	10. whiz	j.	dishes

As you read this paragraph, underline the onomatopoetic words.

We heard people <u>crunching</u> through the snow as they passed our house. A train <u>rumbled</u> by, its <u>clanging</u> bell loud in the stillness of the winter night. My little brother began to <u>whimper</u>; so I read to him his favorite story about a duck chasing a cat away from her ducklings by her loud <u>quacking</u>. Finally Tommy went to sleep, and all was quiet except for the <u>ticking</u> of the grandfather clock.

Challenger

For each of the following, give at least one onomatopoetic word not already mentioned in this lesson.

1. car horn _____ *beep, honk, etc.* _____

2. cars on the highway _____ *zip, zoom, etc.* _____

A Tranquil Scene

In addition to the words we "hear," there are words we "see." Most of the words in bold type below help create visual images.

> The farmer's cattle are **browsing** in the meadow. A rabbit, startled by the shadow of a hawk, **scampers** for safety under a boulder. Nearby, a ground squirrel emerges from his hole, looks about **furtively,** and begins to eat. A lizard suns himself on a warm rock, looking as **inert** as the rock itself. The wild flowers have attracted a **myriad** of butterflies. A shaft of sunlight breaks through a **rift** in the clouds and changes the dark green to bright green. A **prolific** wild apple tree provides food for birds and for animals, both **domesticated** and wild. Such a **tranquil** scene is restful, a good place to spend a quiet afternoon. Some artists and poets like to portray **bucolic** life rather than the life of towns and cities.

Write the words that are defined, choosing from those in bold type.

rift	a.	a narrow opening; a breaking in friendship
domesticated	b.	tame, adapted to life associated with man
browse/browsing	c.	nibble on, or graze; read casually, skim
tranquil	d.	free from disturbance, calm, serene
scamper/scampers	e.	run or leave hastily
prolific	f.	producing in great abundance
bucolic	g.	rustic, characteristic of country life
inert	h.	unable to move; slow to move or act
myriad	i.	*noun,* a vast number; *adj.,* innumerable
furtively	j.	stealthily, slyly, sneakily

Write three sentences of your own, using any three of the words defined above.

Answers will vary.

_____

_____

_____

_____

The finest words in the world are only vain sounds,
if you cannot comprehend them.
—Anatole France (French novelist)

Three

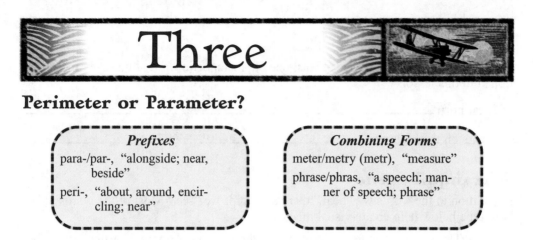

Perimeter or Parameter?

> **Prefixes**
> para-/par-, "alongside; near, beside"
> peri-, "about, around, encircling; near"

> **Combining Forms**
> meter/metry (metr), "measure"
> phrase/phras, "a speech; manner of speech; phrase"

In the lists of word parts, parenthesized forms show the original Greek spellings.

Use the word parts above to make the words that are defined below. Remember that in etymological definitions the root meaning usually precedes the prefix meaning.

paragraph	1.	write beside
paraphrase	2.	phrase beside
periphrasis	3.	phrase around
parameter	4.	measure beside
perimeter	5.	measure around

Of course you know what a **paragraph** is, but the original meaning differed from the present meaning. The word story below explains this difference. For the other four words, which are less familiar, here are explanations.

paraphrase To paraphrase something is to put your own meaning "beside" the original, that is, to state the author's meaning in your own words.

periphrasis (pə-rǐf´rə-sǐs) To use periphrasis is to use a wordy rather than a simple way of saying something—to take the long way around.

Periphrasis (wordiness)	_Direct wording_
the person who owns the ranch	the ranch owner
the baying canine	the hound

parameter This technical mathematical term is best explained in an advanced math class; therefore you need not learn its meaning now. You may hear or see *parameter* in other contexts, used to mean "limits; boundary." (Most of the usage consultants for the *American Heritage Dictionary* do not approve this nontechnical use of the word.)

perimeter The perimeter is the length of the boundary around an area or the outer limits of the area.

Other common words containing the *para-/par-* prefix are *parenthesis, parallel, parable, paralegal,* and *paramedic.* Can you see in each of these words that something or someone is "beside" something or someone else? The Holy Spirit is the *Paraclete* ("called alongside"). A *paraclete* among the ancient Greeks was "one who, as a friend, would plead a person's cause before a judge." Our God is not far off and unreachable. In the person of the Holy Spirit, He is our friend who pleads for us (Rom. 8:26).

Challenger

Give the name of each of these devices.

speedometer	measures the speed of a vehicle
barometer	measures air pressure; useful in predicting weather

Words from Biology

The words in bold type below, though used here in scientific contexts, are not scientific words. Decide what the words mean as they are used here.

1. Men have classified living creatures, but not every **criterion** used in the classification process is trouble free.
2. **Perennial** plants grow year after year.
3. For anything to remain alive, it must maintain a delicate balance of operations. Without this balance, it loses its **equilibrium** and dies.
4. In Mendel's experiments with genetics, he crossed a tall plant with a short one. He called the offspring the first **filial** generation.
5. There were a number of plants, now **extinct,** that looked different from ones with which we are familiar.
6. Darwin's theories are **compatible** with communism, which teaches that through collective effort man can improve his existence.

For each definition, write the correct word found in bold type above.

extinct	a.	not existing in living form now; no longer in use
criterion	b.	a standard or test by which a decision can be made
compatible	c.	capable of acting in harmony with another
equilibrium	d.	a state of balance between opposing forces; a state of adjustment between opposing influences
filial	e.	pertaining to a son or a daughter
perennial	f.	lasting for several years; perpetual; appearing again and again

Here are some additional facts about two of the new words.

Perennial comes from *per-,* "through," and *annus,* "year(s)."

Filial can be used thus: "A child owes filial love to his parents."

In sentences of your own, use any four of the words defined above.

Answers will vary.

_____

_____

One understands a word much better if one has met it alive, in its native habitat.

—C. S. Lewis (English novelist)

Four

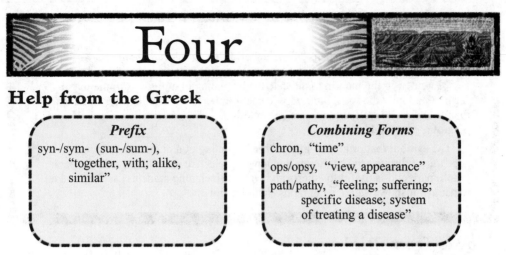

Help from the Greek

> **Prefix**
>
> syn-/sym- (sun-/sum-),
>   "together, with; alike,
>   similar"

> **Combining Forms**
>
> chron, "time"
> ops/opsy, "view, appearance"
> path/pathy, "feeling; suffering;
>   specific disease; system
>   of treating a disease"

The parenthesized word parts are original Greek spellings. Remember that *u* changes to *y* when a Greek word part is used in an English word. Also remember that an *o* is often added to the first of two combining forms: for example, *chronometer*.

Fill in the etymological meanings where spaces occur, using the meanings of the new word parts and some review word parts.

1. **pathos**, "a quality that arouses sympathy or pity" (Since this whole word came from Greek, it is called a Greek *loan word*. It consists of the root *path* and ending *-os*.)

2. **pathetic**, "causing pity or sympathy because of misfortune or inadequacy"

3. **sympathy**, _____ *"feeling together"* _____

4. **telepathy**, _____ *"feeling far off"* _____

5. **naturopathy**, _____ *"system of treating disease by nature"* _____

6. **metric**, "pertaining to the standard of measurement based on the decimal system"

7. **symmetry**, _____ *"measure together"* _____

8. **chronometer**, _____ *"measure time"* _____

9. **synopsis**, _____ *"view together"* _____

In each blank write the word chosen from those above in bold type that could logically introduce the following phrase.

1. _____ *sympathy* _____ for another person, resulting from shared feelings

2. _____ *synopsis* _____ of the plot, presented for a quick view of the story

3. _____ *symmetry* _____ in the design of the Navajo rug

4. _____ *chronometer* _____ of such exceptional preciseness that people set their watches by it

5. _____ *pathetic* _____ situation of the starving children

6. _____ *telepathy* _____ between two people, claimed but not proved

7. _____ *metric* _____ system of weights and measures, official in many countries

8. _____ *naturopathy* _____ with its natural remedies, such as diet, exercise, and sunshine

9. _____ *pathos* _____ in the story, causing her to cry

Let the combining of word parts help you with spelling. For example, notice the reason for the two *ms* in *symmetry.*

Challenger

The Greek prefix *a-* means "without." If Geneva's friends are concerned about her

apathy, what does she seem to lack? _____ *feeling/emotion* _____

Read with Understanding

We must understand words if we are to understand content. God requires of us, "Be ye not unwise, but understanding what the will of the Lord is" (Eph. 5:17). Of course beyond a mental grasp of what we read in the Bible, we need spiritual understanding; only the Holy Spirit can give this.

From context, try to discover the meaning of the words in bold type in the Bible verses below.

1. The great need for food caused some to complain, "We have mortgaged our lands, vineyards, and houses, that we might buy corn, because of the **dearth"** (Neh. 5:3).

2. Seldom does a man willingly accept undeserved suffering, but "Moses, when he was come to years, refused to be called the son of Pharaoh's daughter; choosing rather to suffer **affliction** with the people of God, than to enjoy the pleasures of sin for a season" (Heb. 11:24-25).

3. "And the men that held Jesus mocked him, and smote him. And when they had blindfolded him, they struck him on the face, and asked him, saying, Prophesy, who is it that smote thee? And many other things **blasphemously** spake they against him" (Luke 22:63-65).

4. "And when he had so said, there arose a **dissension** between the Pharisees and the Sadducees: and the multitude was divided" (Acts 23:7).

5. "Now I Nebuchadnezzar praise and **extol** and honour the King of heaven" (Dan. 4:37).

In each blank write the letter for the item that correctly answers the question, using the contexts of the words in bold type to help you.

_____*b*_____ 1. Why did the children of Israel in Nehemiah's day have to mortgage their property?
    a. because there was a war going on
    b. because the corn did not grow

_____*b*_____ 2. Instead of the luxuries and privileges of life with the royal family, what did Moses choose?
    a. temporary exile from Egypt
    b. suffering among his own people

_____*b*_____ 3. Why are the words that the men spoke called *blasphemous?*
    a. because the men interrupted Christ as He spoke
    b. because they were spoken against Christ

_____*a*_____ 4. What happened when he (Paul) spoke?
    a. There was strife between the Pharisees and Sadducees.
    b. The Pharisees and Sadducees agreed about what he said.

_____*a*_____ 5. How did Nebuchadnezzar express his attitude toward the King of heaven?
    a. with three words having similar meaning
    b. by making himself equal to the King of heaven

The important thing about any word is how you understand it.
—Publilius Syrus (Writer of Latin epigrams)

Five

Compounds

Through the combining of prefixes and roots, the English language has acquired a multitude of words. You have found a few of these word parts in previous lessons. Another way of making new words is by forming compounds out of two or more words. This can be done in three different ways, and only by checking a recent dictionary can you be sure which of these ways is right for any particular compound.

1. Words written separately but treated as a unit: trade school, snake in the grass
2. Hyphenated words: after-hours, know-how, good-for-nothing
3. Words written solid: aftermath, backlog, layoff, Newfoundland

Parts of speech combine in a variety of ways to form compounds.

1. noun + prepositional phrase: bill of sale
2. adjective + prepositional phrase: good-for-nothing
3. verb + adverb: layoff
4. preposition + noun: after-hours

In *aftermath* the word *math* is unrelated to our present word *math;* it comes instead from an Old English word meaning "mowing." Today *aftermath* rarely refers to a second cutting of hay. The meaning of *cheapskate* also differs greatly from the apparent meaning based on the parts.

The context of each compound in bold type below suggests its meaning. After reading the paragraph, explain what each compound seems to mean.

In the **aftermath** of the factory **layoff,** Mr. Thomas is one of several unemployed workers whose financial resources are diminishing. He has only a small **backlog** of savings in the bank. He has had the **backbone** to resist his desire for items that he cannot afford. As his family's **breadwinner,** he has provided well but not extravagantly. A few neighbors call him a **cheapskate** because his family lacks some of the luxuries that are often considered necessities. However, being free from debt gives the Thomas family peace of mind.

1. aftermath _____ *results of a misfortune or disaster* _____
2. layoff _____ *shutdown that results in loss of work for employees, at least temporarily*
3. backlog _____ *supply kept in reserve* _____
4. backbone _____ *strong character; determination to do right* _____
5. breadwinner _____ *person who earns the money to provide for his family* _____
6. cheapskate _____ *person who doesn't pay his fair share* _____

Answers will vary.

Blends and Other Words

In addition to compounds, we have *blends,* words made by telescoping two words into one. Blends provide us some fascinating, vivid expressions.

1. A **transistor** is "a device for transferring an electric signal across a resistor"—*trans(fer) + (res)istor.* Transistors greatly improved radio reception.

2. To **don** is to "put on," as a piece of clothing—*do + on.* Don your "Sunday best" for the concert.

3. To **doff** is to "put off," as one's hat—*do + off.* Doff your hat and stay awhile.

4. A **squiggle** is a "wiggly mark or an illegible line"—*squ(irm) + (w)iggle.* Squiggles sometimes pass for signatures.

5. To **squawk** is to "make a loud, harsh sound in protest" (the word can also be a noun)—*squall + squeak.* Officials expect squawks against stricter traffic regulations.

Blends are constantly being formed. Some are not common enough to be included in most dictionaries yet—such as *plumcot* (plum + apricot) and *slanguage* (slang + language).

From the examples above, have you discovered how blends are generally formed? Usually the first part of one word joins the last part of another.

Try making blends from these words. One part in each is not shortened.

___*happenstance*___	1.	happen + circumstance
___*Amerindian*___	2.	American + Indian

To conclude this lesson, you will need five more words. Note them in these sentences.

> In their **quest** for happiness, people may lack concern for the happiness of others. Some have no **qualms** about what their own search for happiness may cost someone else. They **spurn** suggestions about seeking worthwhile goals. Such people **delude** themselves into thinking happiness is the greatest good. Our Lord **exhorts** us, "Seek ye first the kingdom of God, and his righteousness; and all these things shall be added unto you" (Matt. 6:33).

In the space provided, write the word that matches the definition. Choose from the words in bold type above.

___*delude*___	a.	mislead or deceive
___*quest*___	b.	act of seeking; an adventurous search
___*spurn*___	c.	reject disdainfully; scorn
___*exhort*___	d.	earnestly urge to action; make a strong appeal
___*qualm*___	e.	sudden feeling of doubt; pang of conscience

Write three sentences of your own, using any three of the words defined in the exercise above.

1. _____*Answers will vary.*_____

2. _____

3. _____

For the ear trieth [tests] words, as the mouth tasteth meat [food].
—Job 34:3

11

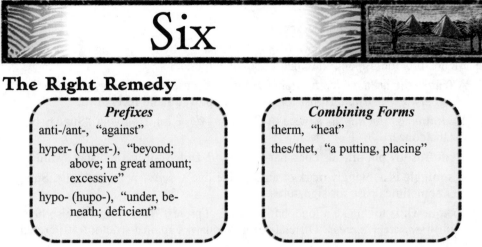

Six

The Right Remedy

> **Prefixes**
> anti-/ant-, "against"
> hyper- (huper-), "beyond; above; in great amount; excessive"
> hypo- (hupo-), "under, beneath; deficient"

> **Combining Forms**
> therm, "heat"
> thes/thet, "a putting, placing"

Occasionally, as in numbers 1 and 2 below, the word parts in an etymological meaning are given in the same order as in the English word, rather than in the usual reverse order.

Write the etymological meaning for each of the words below. (You will be reviewing *syn-/sym-* from Lesson 4.)

1. **hyperthermia,** "unusually high fever" ___excessive heat___

2. **hypothermia,** "subnormal body temperature" ___deficient heat___

3. **hypothesis, hypothetical,** "supposition used as a basis for discussion or investigation" ___a putting under___

4. **antithesis, antithetical,** "the exact opposite" ___a putting against___

5. **synthesis, synthetic,** "the combining of parts to form a whole"
   ___a putting together___

6. **thermometer,** "instrument for measuring temperature" ___measure heat___

To complete these sentences, choose from the words in bold type above.

1. The nurses were busy around the clock. One patient was suffering from ___hypothermia___ after being stranded several hours in a blizzard.

2. In the next room a child was suffering from ___hyperthermia___ , and the ice packs had to be checked frequently.

3. Another patient had bathed his frostbitten hands in hot water; his attempted remedy was the ___antithesis___ of proper medical procedure.

4. People unaccustomed to severe cold may take for granted the false ___hypothesis___ that heat is the remedy for frozen body tissue.

5. The hospital keeps medicines for nearly every ailment; most of the medicines consist of a ___synthesis___ of several ingredients.

Challenger

Give the etymological meaning of *antipathy*.

___feeling against___

In Spite of Fear

Decide from context what the words in bold type mean.

Colonists in the New World had experiences that made even stout-hearted men **quaver.** In our imagination we may picture all pioneers as brave men and women whom danger could not **daunt.**

Colonists did not **relish** the dangers of the wilderness any more than we would have. Generally it was a **fervent** desire for freedom that made colonists willing to face unknown dangers. Trusting in God can **allay** fear today, just as it did for Christians who braved the dangers of the American wilderness.

In the puzzle you will find a synonym for each of the words in bold type. Each of the synonyms forms a right angle in the puzzle, starting vertically and then turning a corner and continuing horizontally to the right. Draw a line around each word that you find, and then complete the matching question below.

```
T  N  Z  R  L  C  R  D  T  Y  B
R  E  M  B  L  E  E  X  B  F  G
H  E  S  D  G  K  L  I  E  V  E
S  N  N  X  Z  D  L  Y  F  Q  Z
N  J  O  Y  K  I  I  S  J  D  B
I  R  D  N  O  S  M  A  Y  D  Y
N  T  E  N  S  E  C  K  R  L  X
```

Write the synonyms for these new words, using the contexts as your clues. The synonyms in the puzzle should be familiar to you.

tremble	1.	quaver
dismay	2.	daunt
enjoy	3.	relish
intense	4.	fervent
relieve	5.	allay

Write sentences of your own, using any four of the words in bold type found in this lesson.

1. _____ *Answers will vary.* _____

2. _____

3. _____

4. _____

If a book that is a classic seems full of hard words, consider that it became a classic because readers understood it; you too will understand it as you expand your vocabulary and the number of hard words diminishes.

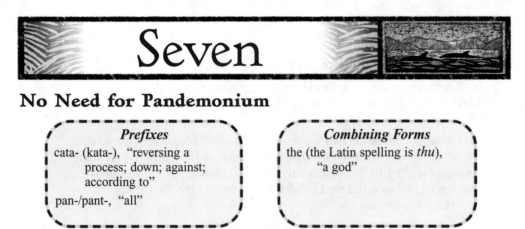

Seven

No Need for Pandemonium

> **Prefixes**
> cata- (kata-), "reversing a process; down; against; according to"
> pan-/pant-, "all"

> **Combining Forms**
> the (the Latin spelling is *thu*), "a god"

The two prefixes in this lesson combine with many Greek roots, of which you are asked to learn only one, *the/thu* (unrelated to the English word *the*).

Notice that the Greek *k* becomes *c* in English derivatives.

Let's begin with three English words having the prefix *cata-*. The etymological meanings are in parentheses.

cataclysm ("to wash down"), "any violent upheaval, such as a flood; catastrophe"

catalog ("to list"), *noun,* "a list with descriptive comments"; *verb,* "make such a list"

catapult ("to hurl down"), *noun,* "ancient military machine for hurling weapons; device for launching aircraft"; *verb,* "throw or launch"

Here are four words beginning with the prefix *pan-/pant-*.

pantheon (*pan + theon,* "all gods"), "all the gods of a people; a building to commemorate all the great persons of a nation; (capitalized), a temple in ancient Rome for all the Roman gods"

panacea ("all cure"), "a supposed cure-all for diseases or difficulties"

panorama ("all view"), "an unlimited view of a wide area"

pandemonium ("all demons"), "wild uproar and confusion"

In front of each item, write the word chosen from those in bold type that fits logically at the beginning of the phrase.

1. _____catalog_____ listing all recorded earthquakes

2. _____pandemonium_____ among panic-stricken people after the earthquake

3. _____panorama_____ of the ruined city, as seen from the top of a hill nearby

4. _____catapult_____ used in World War II to make air attacks from ships

5. _____cataclysm_____ resulting in the death of 600,000 people

6. _____pantheon_____ containing statues of America's heroes and tributes to their achievements

7. _____panacea_____ for all our economic problems, promised by the candidate

Earthquakes

In addition to the words you have just studied, you will need these three words to complete the sentences below.

crucial "of greatest importance in a crisis; severe, difficult"

hazardous "dangerous, risky; depending on chance"

succumb "yield to a superior force or overpowering desire"

To complete the sentences, choose from the words in bold type. One word should be used twice. Use past verb forms or plural nouns if necessary.

1. It is _____hazardous_____ to be near a building during an earthquake.

2. If you reenter your house because you _____succumb_____ to the desire to save your valuables, you are taking a great risk.

3. In 1556, an earthquake in China killed 800,000 people; in terms of lives lost, this was one of the greatest _____cataclysms_____ in recorded history.

4. Scientists _____catalog_____ earthquakes under six headings: great, major, strong, moderate, light, and minor.

5. Using aerial photographs, scientists can study the _____panorama_____ of an area affected by an earthquake.

6. Earth tremors during an earthquake often cause debris from tall buildings to be _____catapulted_____ to the ground.

7. One writer who experienced the 1964 quake in Anchorage, Alaska, tells of the lack of _____pandemonium_____ ; instead, most of the people he observed stood about in stunned silence.

8. As quickly as possible, organizations such as the Red Cross provide such _____crucial_____ assistance as temporary shelter and medical help.

9. God used an earthquake to release Paul and Silas when they were unjustly imprisoned at Philippi. The gods of the Roman _____pantheon_____ had no such power, as the jailer and the magistrates well knew.

10. We who know the Lord can be assured that He is with us even in nature's _____cataclysms_____ ; for He said, "I will never leave thee, nor forsake thee" (Heb. 13:5).

A Major Shift

In Old French, *empestrer* meant "to hobble." The French, like the ancient Romans, would hobble their horses (put a restricting device on the horses' legs) to allow them to pasture but to prevent them from wandering away. This verb obviously came from the Latin noun *pastura*, "pasture." Our modern word *pester* speaks of the annoyance to the horses rather than the pasture where they grazed.

A blow with a word strikes deeper than a blow with a sword.
—Robert Burton (English clergyman and author)

Eight

"The Celestial Railroad"

As you read these paragraphs based on Hawthorne's "Celestial Railroad," pay special attention to the words in bold type. Read through all the sentences carefully before answering the questions that follow.

Nathaniel Hawthorne (1804–1864) was a writer of novels and short stories. He was a **contemporary** of Abraham Lincoln (1809–1865). In his story "The Celestial Railroad," Hawthorne sought to **dispel** some absurd teachings that liberal preachers were presenting. Contrary to common sense, these preachers were presenting the **preposterous** idea that books about morality and philosophy are the remedy for discouragement.

There are an **appreciable** number of similarities between John Bunyan's *Pilgrim's Progress* and "The Celestial Railroad." One similarity is the use of allegory to **portray** a Christian's temptations along the journey to the Celestial City. In Hawthorne's story the narrator's enjoyment of Vanity Fair (an allegorical picture of worldly pleasures) nearly **obliterates** his thoughts of the Celestial City.

Hawthorne also uses satire. For example, Beelzebub's bargaining for a soul is described as something enjoyable to watch, but the reader is expected to make the opposite **inference**. Some of Hawthorne's attacks on the liberals' preaching seem almost **caustic.**

From Hawthorne's fiction we can see how the heresy of liberalism misleads people. In a dramatic way this allegory shows the effects of liberal preaching, and it can help readers **discriminate** between liberalism and truth.

Write the letter for the item that explains or defines the new vocabulary word.

_c_ 1. contemporary
  a. person with the same kind of education
  b. person who does the same kind of work
  c. person living at the same time

_a_ 2. dispel
  a. drive away
  b. support
  c. understand

_b_ 3. preposterous
  a. new
  b. contrary to common sense
  c. unpopular

_a_ 4. appreciable
  a. noticeable
  b. small
  c. exaggerated

_b_ 5. portray
  a. resist
  b. describe
  c. argue against

_a_ 6. obliterate
  a. blot out
  b. repeat
  c. record

_c_ 7. inference
  a. decision to make a purchase
  b. recommendation to the narrator
  c. conclusion from evidence

_b_ 8. caustic
  a. casual
  b. sharp, cutting
  c. occasional

_c_ 9. heresy
  a. inherited beliefs
  b. orthodox teaching
  c. false doctrine

_b_ 10. discriminate
  a. move
  b. distinguish
  c. raise questions

Other Contexts

From the words in bold type, choose the one that can logically introduce each phrase, and write it in the space provided.

1. _____preposterous_____ statement that no one believed

2. _____appreciable_____ improvement over his previous record

3. _____portray_____ the events in vivid language

4. _____heresy_____ that must be exposed in the light of God's Word

5. _____contemporary_____ author, only two years older

6. _____dispel_____ all doubts about his qualifications for the job

7. _____caustic_____ remark that hurt his brother's feelings

8. _____obliterate_____ my name completely from the flyleaf of the book

9. _____inference_____ drawn from his remarks

10. _____discriminate_____ between blue-green and blue

In the puzzle the new words are horizontal and their meanings are vertical. Each new word shares one letter with its meaning. In a few instances the meaning you find will be different from the one derived from the context earlier in this lesson.

```
H E R E S Y O Z S Y Z H Y X I N F E R E N C E N D
E S R Y E K L M N U Q S T E Z N P I N A L O Q R I
T P U S O I C Y A O N F G R L O M N W T Z N M F F
E I Y Z E P L R V N D G H A W A M P Q R S C T E E
R Q T S R V W N M P Q L D S F G H J K L M L N D R
O A T R O B L I T E R A T E N Q D A P N V U L K E
D S T V A B C N D F N V W X B D N B R T N S A G N
O T J H O D P R E P O S T E R O U S T N M I Q P T
X I Q L X F G H Q N E X N V T S N U K L N O Z Y I
Y C P R M N D F H K N V Q G J N S R J Z V N W D A
G N L K A S T E N Z U B D F G H J D K M D B Q P T
L J K N Y V D N O N P R S N D I Q N M F G Q T S E
C O N T E M P O R A R Y G D I S C R I M I N A T E
D N D Q R O L S R O L M M Z Y H K L N R D N J M Y
S B F H K D G J A P P R E C I A B L E N Q L S Z R
A Q Z P Y E G P N K M B A A L D J H T S Q R C N G
R G J B F R C I G N A Z S Q H M V N L S W Q A P N
C P A N V N D C R K L D U O G K L M D V W N T B D
A K L Y D N D T K N V S R F B C N Q D V N X T C K
S K J E B N R U Q J M B A Z T S L M D I S P E L M
T L K P O R T R A Y N Z B F R D Q X Z Y C D R N P
I B Q Y D G K E B N V M L D Q P N S R N Q D G P N
C A U S T I C R N U H N E M D T R H N N R K N I Z
```

Every idle word that men shall speak, they shall give account thereof in the day of judgment.

—Matthew 12:36

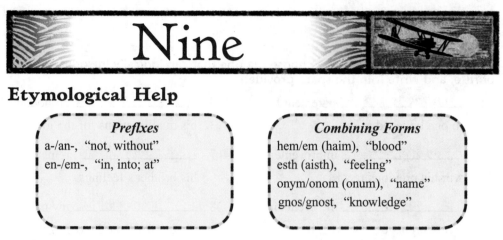

Nine

Etymological Help

> **Prefixes**
> a-/an-, "not, without"
> en-/em-, "in, into; at"

> **Combining Forms**
> hem/em (haim), "blood"
> esth (aisth), "feeling"
> onym/onom (onum), "name"
> gnos/gnost, "knowledge"

Does the Greek prefix *a-* look familiar to you? In Level B of this series is the Latin prefix *a-/ab-/abs-*. From the context of a word having one of these prefixes, you will probably know whether the prefix means "not, without" (Greek) or "away from" (Latin).

The two forms for "blood" *(hem/em)* show that a Greek *h* sometimes disappears in English derivatives. Notice also that the diphthong (combination of two vowels) *ai* changes to the single vowel *e* in English words.

In the following words, the *a-/an-* prefix combines with a root and a suffix. Some of the etymological meanings give the prefix meaning before the root meaning.

anemia, anemic	("without blood")
anesthesia, anesthetic	("without feeling")
anonymous, anonymity	("without a name")
agnostic	("without knowledge [of God]")

The next words combine a new prefix with the roots *path* (Lesson 4), *the/thu,* and two other roots that you are not asked to learn.

atheist, atheism	(*a-* + *the,* "without a god")
abyss, abysmal	(*a-* + *byss,* "without a bottom")
energy	(*en-* + *erg,* "at work")
enthusiasm	(*en-* + *thu,* "a god in")
empathy	(*em-* + *path,* "a feeling in")

In most of the definitions below, a word is missing. Use the etymological meanings to complete these definitions. The first answer is given for you.

1. **anemia,** "deficiency of oxygen-bearing material in the _____*blood*_____"

2. **anemic,** "weak and pale as a result of anemia; lacking vitality"

3. **anesthesia,** "loss of _____*feeling*_____ or consciousness, or both, caused by anesthetic"

4. **anesthetic,** "substance that causes unconsciousness or loss of _____*feeling*_____ , or both"

5. **anonymous,** "by an author whose _____*name*_____ either is not known or is withheld"

6. **agnostic,** "a person who says that the existence of God can __*not*__ be __*known*__ "

7. **atheist,** "a person who disbelieves or denies the existence of _____*God*_____ "

8. **abyss,** "a bottomless or immeasurably deep pit or gulf"

9. **abysmal,** "extreme; immeasurably bad"

18

10. **empathy,** "act of participating or the ability to participate in another person's _____feelings_____ or thoughts"

With the new word parts you are learning, you can recognize the basic meaning of many more words. Here are a few words made from the combining forms in this lesson. The English meaning is given for the words that are probably new to you.

antonym	("name against")
synonym	("name together")
homonym	("name same")
onomatopoeia	("make name") (Note the _o_ added to _onomat._)
pseudonym	("false name"), "an author's fictitious name; pen name"
prognosis	("know before"), "forecast of the probable course and outcome of a disease"

Giddy or Enthusiastic?

In Old English the adjective _gidig_ meant "possessed by a god; mad, crazy." In Middle English the spelling changed to _gidy._ Today _giddy_ has softened to mean "dizzy; lighthearted, frivolous, or silly."

The ancient Greeks also believed that a person possessed by a god was mad. Their word was _enthousiasmos_ from _en-_ + _theos,_ "a god in." Our words _enthusiasm_ and _giddy_ have lost their association with pagan religion and no longer have similar meanings. If someone mentions your enthusiasm, you have received a compliment; if, on the other hand, someone calls you giddy, you may need to be more sensible or serious-minded.

Without Belief

Choose words from all those in bold type to complete the sentences.

1. Thomas Huxley was an _____agnostic_____ who believed in evolution. He took as his motto concerning God "not proven."

2. Karl Marx, an _____atheist_____, denied the existence of God.

3. Marx declared, "Religion is the opium of the people." Opium, like an _____anesthetic_____, causes sleepiness; but true faith in Christ gives believers a zeal to serve their Lord.

4. Men like Marx show an _____abysmal_____ lack of understanding of God's Word.

5. In the bottomless pit, or _____abyss_____, unbelievers will spend eternity (Rev. 20:3).

6. Christians, remembering their own years of unbelief, should have an _____empathy_____ for unbelievers and a desire to see them saved.

7. Like the Apostle Paul, a person who knows Christ should boldly speak and perhaps write what Christ has done for him—not timidly as a(n) _____anonymous_____ Christian using a _____pseudonym_____.

God's Word is like Himself, "the same yesterday, today, and forever."
—Robert Payne Smith (English theologian)

Ten

Versatile Word Parts

> **Combining Forms**
>
> dog/dox, "opinion, teaching; accepted teaching"
> phile/phil, "love for; one who loves or likes"
> crypt, "hidden"
> astr/aster, "star; star-shaped; pertaining to outer space"
> log/logue, "word; speech; reason"

Some Greek word parts are versatile: they may be used at the beginning, middle, or end of a word. Notice the various uses of the word parts in this lesson.

Underline the Greek combining forms that are defined above.

dog<u>matic</u>   <u>logical</u>   <u>phil</u>o<u>sopher</u>

ortho<u>dox</u>   epi<u>logue</u>   <u>Phil</u>adelphia   <u>crypt</u>ic

hetero<u>dox</u>   pro<u>logue</u>   biblio<u>phile</u>

ana<u>log</u>ous

Did you notice the *o* added to the first of the two combining forms in *orthodox, heterodox, philosopher,* and *bibliophile?*

Both the etymological meaning and the present meaning are given for these words. Five of the words have the accent marked to help you pronounce them correctly.

dogmat´ic	("opinion, belief"), "authoritative in stating a truth or belief; arrogant in stating something that is unproved or unprovable"
or´thodox	("right opinion"), "following the accepted or established belief"
het´erodox	("another opinion"), "unorthodox, departing from or contrary to accepted beliefs"
philosopher	("lover of wisdom"), "a person who loves and seeks wisdom"
Philadelphia	("brotherly love"), "a city in Pennsylvania; an ancient city in Asia Minor" (Rev. 3:7–13)
bib´liophile	("love books"), "a person who loves or collects books"
logical	("speech, word, reason"), "reasonable; able to reason clearly"
epilogue	("word upon or in addition"), "a short concluding section of a literary work; final speech in some plays, spoken directly to the audience"
prologue	("word before"), "lines introducing a literary work"
anal´ogous	("word according to"), "similar or alike in some ways"
cryptic	("hidden"), "hidden; secret, mysterious; puzzling"

Before each statement write the appropriate word from the list above.

Philadelphia   1. People who live there should be friendly.

cryptic   2. The secret message was hard to understand.

orthodox   3. Their beliefs agree with the Bible; they accept the Bible as their authority in all things.

heterodox   4. A faithful pastor would point out how these religious systems differ from Bible teaching.

analogous   5. Our principal showed us that our grades were like a crop that a farmer harvests.

logical   6. His statement shows clear thought and good judgment.

dogmatic   7. It is unwise to sound authoritative without the facts.

Challengers

To answer these questions, use the etymological meanings you have learned.

1. What shape does an *asterisk* have? _____ star _____

2. What flower gets its name from its star shape? _____ aster _____

3. What would a *cryptographer* do? _write in secret code/write things with a_ _hidden meaning_

The Bibliophile

To complete these sentences, choose from the words in bold type.

1. Tim is a _____ bibliophile _____ who especially enjoys his job in the library.

2. People from his church, wanting books that will build them up in the faith, often ask him whether a particular book is orthodox or _____ heterodox _____ .

3. A college student studying ancient history asked Tim about the beliefs of Socrates, Plato, Pythagoras, and other ancient _____ philosophers _____ best known for their desire for wisdom.

4. One student wanted help in finding a story with a theme _____ analogous _____ to that of *Treasure Island*.

5. Tim helped a literature student find a copy of *Romeo and Juliet*. The student was to find the main events of the play, as stated in the _____ prologue _____ .

6. Another student was looking for Prospero's final speech, which is the _____ epilogue _____ of *The Tempest*.

Every living language . . . is in perpetual motion . . . ; some words go off,
and become obsolete; others are taken in, and by degrees grow into common
use; or the same word is inverted to a new sense and notion.

—Richard Bentley (English cleric and scholar)

Eleven

Clipped Words

We tend to clip many long words, keeping just one or two syllables. Write the word from which each clipped word came, being careful to spell each correctly. Use a dictionary if you need to.

advertisement	1.	ad	*gasoline*	4.	gas
examination	2.	exam	*gymnasium*	5.	gym
mathematics	3.	math	*submarine/substitute*	6.	sub

Write the clipped words made from these words.

memo	1.	memorandum	*prof*	3.	professor
sax	2.	saxophone	*curio*	4.	curiosity

Here are some clipped-word origins that may surprise you.

Around 1820, Congressman Walker from Buncombe County, North Carolina, made a foolish speech. Since then foolish or meaningless talk has been called *bunkum* (from the name of his county) or **bunk.**

In *The Canterbury Tales* pilgrims ride to Canterbury to visit a shrine. The name of the town has been shortened to **canter** and refers to the pace at which the horses would travel on this journey.

A **mob** was at first a *mobile vulgus,* Latin for "a changeable or fickle crowd of common people."

Most clipped words are the first syllable(s) of the original words. *Flu* is taken from within *influenza.* Here are a few words that have been clipped from the ends of longer words.

bus	from *omnibus,* "a vehicle for all; also a book containing works that are all by one author or all on one subject"
cab	from *taxicab* (also shortened to *taxi*), "an automobile for public transportation"
van	from **caravan,** "a large covered vehicle; also a group of people traveling single file, as across a desert"
cute	from **acute,** "sensitive; extremely severe or sharp"
drawing room	"a formal reception room," from *withdrawing room,* originally "a room used for sleeping"
wayward	"willful, headstrong, ungovernable," from *awayward,* "turned away"
varsity	"the main college or university team," from *university*

Write original sentences, using the words indicated.

1. caravan _____

Answers will vary.
_____

2. acute _____

_____

3. wayward _____

_____

A Congenial Family

Since most of the clipped words discussed above are probably already in your active vocabulary, you will find only two of them in bold type below. Note how these and the other new words are used in sentences, and try to decide from their contexts what they mean.

Dressed in elegant attire, the duchess sits for her portrait. The painter asks her to remain in a **pensive** mood. The artist has already worked four **consecutive** days on the portrait.

In the evening the duchess relaxes as she and the duke ride through the woods, returning at a **canter** when darkness falls. At the dinner hour they are served a **sumptuous** meal. During dinner their son **enumerates** his day's activities. He is a lad of **indomitable** spirit, always eager to attempt new things and rarely discouraged by failures. The duchess, with her usual **maternal** concern, admonishes him not to take needless risks. As their leisurely meal ends and the **embers** in the fireplace are burning low, we take our leave of this **congenial** family.

In what **era,** you may be wondering, is the setting of this incident? In an **omnibus** of stories about medieval knights, you might find such a scene. Or it might be a modern setting, for there are still dukes and duchesses living on large estates in England.

In each blank write the word that matches the definition. Choose from the words in bold type.

congenial	a.	"harmonious, friendly; pleasant"
maternal	b.	"motherly; related through one's mother"
pensive	c.	"deeply thoughtful, often with sadness"
omnibus	d.	"book of stories on a single theme"
indomitable	e.	"unconquerable, not able to be put down"
canter	f.	"easy pace of a horse, faster than a trot and slower than a gallop"
era	g.	"period of time distinguished by an important event or a characteristic feature"
consecutive	h.	"coming one after another without a break"
sumptuous	i.	"lavish, luxurious"
embers	j.	"glowing coals in the ashes of a dying fire"
enumerate	k.	"count; list or name one by one"

Just a Little Burg

If you live in a small town, you may have been offended by the comment, "Oh, that's just a little burg." There is no reason to be offended, for *burg* is defined today as simply "a city or town." The word came to us from Old English; and up through medieval times, a burg was a castle or a walled town. In its earliest form, the word meant "high" and referred either to hills or to forts.

Some related words are *borough,* *barrow,* Canter*bury,* ice*berg,* and *bourgeois.*

An eloquent man treats humble subjects with delicacy,
lofty things impressively, and moderate things temperately.
—Marcus Tullius Cicero (Roman statesman, orator, author)

Twelve

Historically Speaking

Knowing word meanings makes lesson preparation easier and faster. The sentences below might be used in a history lesson. Notice especially the words in bold type.

1. Because word-of-mouth information can easily be forgotten or **distorted,** men have written down traditions of the past to preserve an accurate record for future generations.

2. From the peoples scattered from the Tower of Babel come the **distinctive** cultures of the past and present.

3. The Bible is historically accurate. The book of Daniel tells about God's warning of **impending** judgment on the king and the city.

4. That very night the seemingly **invincible** city of Babylon fell to the Medes and Persians, and Belshazzar was slain.

5. Whether or not there is always evidence to **confirm** events in the Bible, those events happened just as the Bible says they did.

Context does not always provide enough information for you to discover the exact meaning of a word, so here is more help.

distort	"mislead, misrepresent; twist out of its natural shape"
distinctive	"identifying, distinguishing; characteristic, typical"
impending	"about to take place; hovering threateningly"
invincible	"unconquerable"
confirm	"verify, establish as true"

Using the meanings of the new words, choose the answer that correctly completes the restatement of the five numbered sentences above.

___a___ 1. Oral history is likely to be
   a. less accurate than written history.
   b. handed down by people who are accurate in stating facts.
   c. remembered because of its vividness.

___b___ 2. Since the Tower of Babel, the cultures in various parts of the world have developed
   a. many similarities.
   b. noticeable differences.
   c. in interesting ways.

___c___ 3. Through His prophet Daniel, God told the Babylonians that judgment
   a. would be delayed.
   b. could be avoided.
   c. was at hand.

___a___ 4. The people of Babylon no doubt thought that their city
   a. could not be destroyed.
   b. could not be excelled.
   c. could not be in any serious danger.

___c___ 5. The Bible is true
   a. even though historians may disagree with its statements.
   b. because history proves each event that it records.
   c. whether or not historians can prove it.

Early Civilizations

The following sentences give information about various early civilizations. Try to determine from context the meaning of each word in bold type.

1. More than two thousand years before Christ, a new people moved into Mesopotamia and began to **assert** their own influence upon the cities in which they settled.

2. The sixth king of the Amorites, Hammurabi, is famous for his code of laws. He did not write these laws but **compiled,** organized, and simplified existing laws.

3. Hammurabi's law code was a great improvement over the **capricious** decrees of other ancient kings, but Moses' law, because it was given by God, is far superior to any law code of man.

4. **Comprising** many city-states, Phoenicia was located along the eastern coast of the Mediterranean Sea (where Lebanon is today).

5. The Greeks invented their own gods. These gods reflected man's sinfulness: they were immoral, impatient, **whimsical,** unjust, and deceitful.

Here is help for the new words, in addition to the context help.

assert	"state positively or boldly; declare, affirm"
compile	(Latin, "bundle together"), "bring together from various sources; collect into a single book"
capricious	"impulsive, unpredictable; inclined to sudden changes"
comprise	"include, contain; consist of"
whimsical	(adj. from noun *whimsy*), "unpredictable; imaginative, fanciful"

The scene changes from ancient history to the nineteenth century in Europe and America. To complete the paragraph below, choose from all the words in bold type in this lesson. Use the past verb form if necessary.

The early nineteenth century is known as the Romantic Age. If we should _____*compile*_____ a list of writers during that period in Britain, Europe, and America, most would be Romantics. Such a list would _____*comprise*_____ writers having a wide variety of interests. There is a _____*distinctive*_____ difference between these writers and their immediate predecessors in their attitudes toward government and society. Many Romantics opposed a stable social order; they _____*asserted*_____ that individual liberty was of primary importance. Knowingly or unknowingly, they _____*distorted*_____ the importance of such liberty. One trend during the Romantic Age was to glorify the _____*invincible*_____ spirit of men who struggle to be free. At the time of the French Revolution, the serious consequences of liberty without restraint were _____*impending*_____ ; but the Romantics focused their attention on liberty rather than on the threatening consequences. The events of that revolution _____*confirm*_____ that liberty must be restrained by law. Not all Romantic writing is serious; for example, we find some _____*whimsical*_____ works such as Charles Lamb's *Essays of Elia.*

The words of the Lord are pure words: as silver tried in a furnace of earth, purified seven times.

—Psalm 12:6

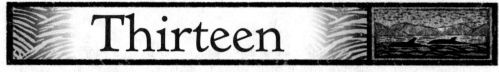

Thirteen

Reduplication

We like the repetition of rhyming words, of rhythm in songs and poems, of the choruses in songs, and of the *rah rah rah* at a ball game. Reduplication of a sound within a word is another kind of repetition that we enjoy. Reduplication usually occurs in one of the following three ways.

Word repeated exactly	*Initial consonant(s) changed*	*Vowel changed*
yum-yum	hubbub	wishy-washy
tut-tut	razzle-dazzle	riffraff

Words made by reduplication are rich in connotation; many of them are informal. You can enrich your vocabulary with some that are new to you.

These three short puzzles illustrate the three kinds of reduplication. For each puzzle, put the words in the same order as the definitions. The hyphen in each word is supplied for you.

chow-chow
tut-tut
tom-tom
ack-ack
hush-hush

1. "an antiaircraft gun"
2. "a vegetable relish pickled in mustard sauce"
3. "a small drum usually beaten with the hands"
4. "secret, very confidential"
5. "an expression of mild annoyance or disapproval"

1. A C K - A C K
2. C H O W - C H O W
3. T O M - T O M
4. H U S H - H U S H
5. T U T - T U T

razzle-dazzle
helter-skelter
harum-scarum
hurly-burly
fuddy-duddy

1. "uproar, turmoil"
2. "old-fashioned person; concerned about details, critical"
3. "confusion or excitement intended to bewilder"
4. "in a hasty, disorderly manner; pell-mell"
5. "reckless"

1. H U R L Y - B U R L Y
2. F U D D Y - D U D D Y
3. R A Z Z L E - D A Z Z L E
4. H E L T E R - S K E L T E R
5. H A R U M - S C A R U M

tittle-tattle
shilly-shally
flip-flop
wishy-washy
fiddle-faddle

1. "backward somersault; abrupt change of opinion or direction"
2. "nonsense; an expression of mild annoyance"
3. "gossip; trivial chatter"
4. "weak, indecisive, lacking strong character"
5. "waste time in indecision about trivial things"

1. F L I P - F L O P
2. F I D D L E - F A D D L E
3. T I T T L E - T A T T L E
4. W I S H Y - W A S H Y
5. S H I L L Y - S H A L L Y

Perhaps through the combined knowledge of your class you can learn the meanings of all the reduplicated words below. First, put a check mark by each reduplicated word that all the class members know well. Then take turns reading the meanings of those that remain and making up sentences to illustrate their use. Check off each word as soon as someone uses it correctly. If time permits, you might include the ones in the puzzles as well as those listed below.

claptrap	"insincere, empty talk"	**namby-pamby**	"weak; indecisive, spineless"
flimflam	"fraud, swindle"	**niminy-piminy**	"affectedly refined, finicky"
higgledy-piggledy	"in disorder, topsy-turvy"	**ragtag**	"low-class people, rabble; ragged, unkempt; sometimes called *ragtag and bobtail*"
hoity-toity	"having false show of importance; condescending"		
hugger-mugger	"disorder, confusion; secrecy"	**riffraff**	"disreputable people, rabble; rubbish"
mishmash	"jumble of unrelated things, hodgepodge"	**willy-nilly**	"willingly or unwillingly; disorganized"

Vivid Words

Vivid descriptions add to reading enjoyment. You can make your own descriptive writing more enjoyable to others if you have a vocabulary well stocked with words that stir the imagination. Add these four to your active vocabulary.

affable	"easy to talk with; friendly, gracious"
dejected	"discouraged, disheartened"
droll	(from Dutch *drol,* "little man"), "comically amusing, odd"
quench	"extinguish; overcome, suppress; satisfy"

Use the four words above to complete these sentences.

1. In a crowd Ben is often the center of attention, amusing others with his
   _____*droll*_____ sense of humor.

2. He is outgoing and _____*affable*_____ , making new friends easily.

3. When he meets a fellow student who looks _____*dejected*_____ , he tries to cheer him up.

4. Ben has a spirit of optimism that discouragement seldom _____*quenches*_____ .

Challenger

In sentences of your own, use *quench* and *affable*.

1. _____*Answers will vary.*_____

   _____

2. _____

   _____

> ### How much is in the budget?
> In Old French a *bouge* was "a leather bag," and a *bougette* was "a little leather bag." A merchant learned how much money he had by opening his *bougette.* In Middle English the word *bouget* meant "a small sack for money."
>
> It would be wise for anyone (or any government) when making a *budget* to follow the example of those medieval French merchants by looking in the *bougette* and spending only the money he actually has.

Memorable sentences are memorable, on account of some single irradiating word.
—Alexander Smith (Scottish poet)

Fourteen

Alligators

William Bartram explored Florida in the late eighteenth century, "invading" lagoons that were the domain of alligators. The following sentences, based on or quoted from a portion of his *Travels,* will give you a hint of the excitement of his adventures. Bartram narrates part of the action in the historical present and part in past tense. If you haven't read this episode, you will probably want to read his own account and find out what happened.

Notice in particular the words in bold type.

Bartram tells us that alligators are shaped like lizards and are covered with scales that not even rifle balls can penetrate, but they are **vulnerable** near the head and just behind the forelegs. "The alligator when full grown is a very large and terrible creature, and of **prodigious** strength, activity, and swiftness in the water."

Bartram begins the narration of one incident by describing his **vantage** point, which was on the "highest part of the ground." From there he could see where a river emptied into a large lagoon, "elegantly **embellished** with flowering plants and shrubs." Two alligators approached each other. As Bartram describes it, "The boiling surface of the lake marks their rapid course, and a terrific conflict **commences.**" He continues, "Again they sink, when the contest ends at the bottom of the lake, and the vanquished makes a hazardous escape, hiding himself in the muddy **turbulent** waters and sedge on a distant shore."

After watching the dreadful battle, Bartram was apprehensive. Especially when he went out in his little boat, he was **vigilant,** keeping "strictly on the watch." His fears were soon confirmed. "My situation now became **precarious** to the last degree. Two very large ones attacked me closely."

One of them followed Bartram to shore. It just lay there, looking at him. Bartram resolved that the alligator should pay for his **temerity;** so he returned to camp to get his gun. He cleared an area around his camp so there would be no **impediment** to hinder him if the alligator should attack at night.

We need to be alert to context clues to the meaning of unfamiliar words. Occasionally clues are in a sentence nearby, rather than in the sentence where the word occurs. Try to find the context clues to the meanings of these words.

In the space provided, write the letter for the helpful sentence portion(s). Where three suggestions are given, there are two right answers.

_a_ 1. vulnerable
    a. "not even rifle balls can penetrate, but . . ."
    b. "when full grown"

_b_ 2. prodigious
    a. "flowering plants and shrubs"
    b. "very large and terrible"

_a, b_ 3. vantage
    a. "he could see"
    b. "highest part of the ground"
    c. "Two alligators"

_a, c_ 4. embellished
    a. "elegantly"
    b. "begins the narration"
    c. "flowering"

_b_ 5. commences
    a. "a hazardous escape"
    b. "approached each other"

_a_ 6. turbulent
    a. "muddy . . . waters and sedge"
    b. "on the distant shore"

_b_ 7. vigilant
    a. "the distant shore"
    b. "strictly on the watch"

_b, c_ 8. precarious
    a. "he should pay"
    b. "attacked me closely"
    c. "to the last degree"

_a_ 9. temerity
    a. "attacked me closely"
    b. "get my gun"

_b_ 10. impediment
    a. "around my camp"
    b. "to hinder me"

Make the Meanings Match

In front of each word, write the letter for the word's meaning.

_g_ 1. vantage   a. "dangerous because of uncertain circumstances"

_c_ 2. embellished   b. "enormous; extraordinary, amazing"

_f_ 3. commence   c. "made beautiful, adorned, with ornamental details"

_d_ 4. turbulent   d. "full of turmoil and disorder; tumultuous"

_i_ 5. impediment   e. "capable of being wounded; open to attack"

_j_ 6. vigilant   f. "start; begin existence"

_a_ 7. precarious   g. "position giving a wide view or an advantage"

_h_ 8. temerity   h. "boldness, rash disregard of danger"

_e_ 9. vulnerable   i. "hindrance, obstacle, obstruction"

_b_ 10. prodigious   j. "alert to avoid danger, watchful"

What People Think of the Bourgeoisie

Originally *bourgeoisie* (plural of *bourgeois*) were people living in walled towns, or *bourgs* (burgs). Gradually *bourgeoisie* came to refer to the middle class. The upper class looked down on them, considering them mediocre; and the lower class resented them for being above the poor. In the nineteenth century followers of Karl Marx opposed them for being property owners. Today *bourgeoisie* means "middle class; people interested mainly in respectability and material values."

Whenever we come upon one of those intensely right words in a book or a newspaper, the resulting effect is . . . electrically prompt.
—Mark Twain (American author and humorist)

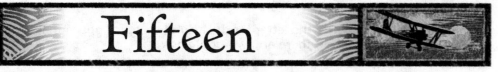

Fifteen

Diminutives and Superlatives

Certain prefixes and suffixes cause words to describe or name diminutive (very small) things or superlative (very large or great) things. We begin with some Greek prefixes that form diminutives and superlatives.

micro-/micr-	"small; abnormally small; one-millionth" (microbe, microphone, microscope)
macro-/macr-	"large; long; inclusive" (macromolecule, macroscopic)
mega-	"large; one million" (megaphone, megabuck, megaton)

Here are the meanings of some that you should learn.

microbe	"germ, minute organism that causes disease" (a general, non-technical term)
macroscopic	"large enough to be seen without a microscope"
megabuck	(slang) "one million dollars"
megaton	"an explosive force equal to a million tons of TNT"

Suffixes also can give words diminutive or superlative meaning. They come from several sources, and some have variant spellings. We begin with examples of diminutive-forming suffixes:

-kin
> manikin (little man)
> Adkins (little Adam)
> Perkins (little Peter)

-et/-ette
> clarinet (little trumpet, Ital., *clarino*)
> kitchenette (little kitchen)
> Jeannette (little Jeanne)

-illo/-illa
> peccadillo (little sin; little fault, Sp., *pecado*)
> guerrilla (little war, Sp., *guerra*)

-el/-cle
> morsel (little bite, Lat., *morsus*)
> muscle (little mouse, Lat., *mus*)

-olus/-ula/-ule
> gladiolus (little sword, Lat., *gladius*)
> capsule (little box, Lat., *capsa*)

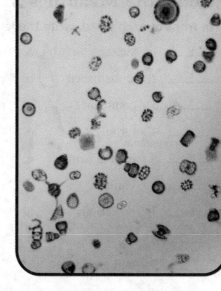

The number of superlative-forming suffixes is much smaller. One that is necessary in reading music is **-issimo**.

pianissimo   (very softly or quietly)   **fortissimo**   (very loudly)

Here is a bit more information about three of the diminutives.

gladiolus	This flower has leaves shaped like little swords.
muscle	A much-exercised muscle looks like a small mouse moving under the skin.
peccadillo	Of course there is no small sin.

To complete the statements below, you need to reason logically.

_____*towelette*_____ 1.   If a small kitchen is a *kitchenette,* what is a small towel?

_____*owlet*_____ 2.   If a piglet is a young pig, what is a young owl?

Watching Pennies

Here are five new words to learn.

cliché	"an overused phrase"
commendable	"worthy of praise"
discrepancy	"difference between a statement and the facts; inconsistency"
frugal	"avoiding unnecessary or wasteful spending; inexpensive; meager"
preferable	"more desirable"

Write the word that fits each context. Remember that context clues can be in nearby sentences. Use plural noun forms if necessary.

Grandma's supper is _____*frugal*_____ . Her avoidance of wasteful spending is _____*commendable*_____ , but her children haven't always understood her thrift. When she was growing up, she says, it was nip and tuck whether her family would have enough to eat, and life was no bed of roses. Often she has to explain her _____*clichés*_____ , especially to her grandchildren. She says that of course a more comfortable life would have been _____*preferable*_____ , but she learned valuable lessons from the hardships.

Choose words from those in bold type to complete these sentences. Use plural noun forms if necessary.

1. Sue and I spent the afternoon in the new shopping mall. As we passed the pet store, we stopped at an aquarium to watch strange tropical fish darting about for _____*morsels*_____ of food.

2. The music store was featuring a pianist in the open mall area. Remarkably, we could hear the music even when he played _____*pianissimo*_____ .

3. In a toy store we found a _____*manikin*_____ that bore a surprising resemblance to my brother.

4. One of my _____*peccadillos*_____ is to overspend on shopping trips, but today's shopping was an exception.

5. Obviously it cost _____*megabucks*_____ to build this mall, and the customers are paying for it.

6. Today I began, for the first time ever, to notice a _____*discrepancy*_____ between the price and the quality of many items.

7. The influence of my mother's _____*frugal*_____ ways sometimes helps me to limit my spending.

8. Though stated in _____*clichés*_____ , her advice is worth remembering: "A person who is hard-pressed for cash shouldn't be in the depths of despair. He should bite the bullet and determine to live within his means."

I will not forget thy word.
—Psalm 119:16

Cumulative Reviews

Review 1

Match the following word parts and their meanings.

_____b_____   1. epi-/ep-   a. distant, far off

_____d_____   2. poly-   b. on, upon; among

_____a_____   3. tele-   c. something written

_____e_____   4. dem   d. many, much

_____c_____   5. gram   e. people

From the words listed choose the correct one to begin each phrase below.

    epidemic   epigram   epigraph   polygraph   telegraph

1. _____epigraph_____ on the tombstone

2. _____epidemic_____ of chicken pox

3. _____polygraph_____ to determine the honesty of a job applicant

4. _____epigram_____ four lines long, ridiculing cowards

5. _____telegraph_____ the message as quickly as possible

Review 2

Complete the following statements with words you learned in Lessons 1 and 2.

1. A word's _____etymology_____ traces that word from its earliest recorded form and meaning up to the present.

2. Any word that has been coined to imitate a particular sound is called a(n) _____onomatopoetic_____ word.

3. To imitate the sound of a fire burning in a fireplace, you could use the word _____crackle_____.

4. To imitate the sound of bacon frying, you could use the word _____sizzle_____.

5. Give another imitative word, and tell what the sound of the word imitates.
   _____*Answers will vary.*_____

Use these words to complete the sentences that follow; use the past verb form and plural nouns if necessary.

    browse   epigram   myriad   tranquil
    concession   furtively   prolific

1. In the library I _____browsed_____ through several books before choosing one to read.

2. Two girls were whispering, looking around _____*furtively*_____ to see whether a librarian was near.

3. Except for occasional whispering, the library is a _____*tranquil*_____ place to read.

4. When I look at _____*myriad*_____ books on the shelves, I often wonder whether all of them are read.

5. The complete works of Charles Dickens amaze me. To read all the books by this _____*prolific*_____ writer would be a major accomplishment.

6. Our English teacher has made a _____*concession*_____ to any student who reads *Bleak House* or another equally long Dickens novel: it will count as two shorter novels for our reading assignment.

7. Before leaving the library, I found the book I was looking for—a collection of _____*epigrams*_____ by a variety of American writers from Benjamin Franklin to Will Rogers.

Review 3

Give the word indicated by each etymological meaning.

_____*telegram*_____	1.	written far off
_____*paraphrase*_____	2.	phrase beside
_____*periphrasis*_____	3.	phrase around
_____*perimeter*_____	4.	measure around

In the space provided write the letter for the meaning of each word.

_i_	1. bucolic	a.	a standard used as the basis for a decision or judgment
_g_	2. compatible	b.	run or leave hastily
_a_	3. criterion	c.	pertaining to a son or a daughter
_h_	4. equilibrium	d.	incapable of moving; slow to move or act
_j_	5. extinct	e.	a narrow opening; a breaking or parting
_c_	6. filial	f.	lasting several years; appearing again and again
_d_	7. inert	g.	capable of acting in harmony with another
_f_	8. perennial	h.	a state of balance between opposing forces
_e_	9. rift	i.	characteristic of country life, rustic
_b_	10. scamper	j.	not used now; nonexistent in living form

33

Combine the word parts to make five of the words that are defined. For the other definition, write a Greek loan word without a prefix.

syn-/sym-	chron	ops/opsy
tele-	meter/metry	path/pathy

chronometer   1.   an instrument, such as a clock, that *measures time*

synopsis   2.   a short summary, making possible a *view of the whole together*

sympathy   3.   a *feeling with* another person, of sorrow, pity, understanding; also of agreement, favor

symmetry   4.   similarity in form, having the same pattern on both sides; *measured alike*

pathos   5.   a quality, such as *suffering,* that arouses sympathy or pity

telepathy   6.   *feelings* sent and felt *afar* (an unproven experience)

Use these words to complete the sentences that follow. Use past verb forms if necessary.

affliction	dissension	pathetic
blasphemously	extol	

1. There seemed to be a constant ___dissension___ between the Pharisees and the Sadducees.

2. As students of the Old Testament, the leaders of Israel should have recognized Christ as the fulfillment of prophecy and should have ___extolled___ Him and His works.

3. Instead, they spoke ___blasphemously___ against Him (Luke 22:65).

4. Isaiah prophesied the ___affliction___ of the Savior: "He was wounded for our transgressions, he was bruised for our iniquities" (Isa. 53:5).

5. The word ___pathetic___ is not appropriate to describe Christ in His suffering, for He did not suffer because of misfortune or inadequacy. Christ willingly laid down His life and had "power to take it again" (John 10:18).

Review 5

Write the letter for the meaning of each word in the space provided.

_c_   1. aftermath   a. a chance circumstance

_d_   2. backbone   b. to remove

_h_   3. breadwinner   c. the results of a misfortune or disaster

_i_   4. cheapskate (slang)   d. strength of character; determination to do right ___g___ 5. don   e. a shutdown resulting in a loss of work for employees

___b___ 6. doff   f. a wiggly mark

___e___ 7. layoff   g. to put on

___f___ 8. squiggle   h. a person who earns money to support his family

___a___ 9. happenstance   i. a stingy person

Captain John Smith's account of the Jamestown colony gives us an insight into the character of the colonists. Choose from the list the correct word to complete each sentence. Use the past verb form if necessary.

dearth   delude   exhort   qualms   quest   spurn

1. Upon their arrival in America, the men of the Virginia Company spent much time in _____quest_____ of gold and pearls.

2. Before setting out for America, they had been _____deluded_____ by reports that gold and jewels lay on top of the ground in the New World.

3. Though the leaders _____exhorted_____ the colonists to build houses, plant crops, and organize the colony's defense, the men _____spurned_____ such practical advice.

4. Without crops, the colonists soon faced a severe _____dearth_____ of food.

5. Unexplainably, the Indians began to bring food; the colonists accepted it with no apparent _____qualms_____ .

Review 6

For each etymological meaning write the word that is defined.

_____hyperthermia_____ 1. excessive heat

_____hypothermia_____ 2. deficient heat

_____antithesis_____ 3. a putting against

_____synthesis_____ 4. a putting together

_____thermometer_____ 5. measure heat

Use these words to complete the sentences, changing verb forms if necessary.

allay   daunt   hypothesis   relish
antithesis   fervent   quaver

1. In Poe's "The Masque of the Red Death," the rapid course of the disease caused most onlookers to _____quaver_____ .

2. In spite of this horrid plague, however, Prince Prospero determined not to let the death of half his subjects _____daunt_____ him.

35

3. His _____**fervent**_____ wish to _____**allay**_____ the danger to himself and his friends prompted him to adopt a bold plan.

4. He and a thousand of his friends would withdraw to the safety of a well-guarded abbey, and he _____**relished**_____ the thought that they would be safely shut off from all who were afflicted.

5. After they were shut in, he invited his friends to a masked ball, the very _____**antithesis**_____ of the suffering throughout the rest of his kingdom.

6. The prince's _____**hypothesis**_____ that escape from the Red Death was possible proved to be nothing more than a conjecture.

Review 7

In the space provided write the letter for the definition of each of these words.

_f_	1. cataclysm	a.	throw or launch
_d_	2. catalog	b.	wild uproar and noise
_a_	3. catapult	c.	supposition from which a conclusion is drawn
_g_	4. pantheon	d.	make a systematized list
_e_	5. panacea	e.	cure-all
_h_	6. panorama	f.	catastrophe
_b_	7. pandemonium	g.	a temple for all a nation's gods; a building to honor a nation's great men
_c_	8. hypothesis	h.	unlimited view of a wide area

Choose from these words to complete the sentences, using the past verb form if necessary.

cataclysm   crucial   pandemonium   succumb
catalog   hazardous   panorama   synthesis
catapult   panacea   pantheon

1. In a _____**pantheon**_____ honoring mythical Greek heroes, Ulysses would surely hold a chief place.

2. The end of the Trojan War was a _____**cataclysm**_____ for the Trojans, a victory for the Greeks.

3. Having won the war, the Greeks then had to begin their long and _____**hazardous**_____ journey home.

4. As they sailed away, the bleak _____**panorama**_____ of Troy in ruins looked vastly different from the thriving city they had first seen ten years earlier.

5. From Homer's *Odyssey* one could _____**catalog**_____ the peoples and places the Greeks visited on their long journey.

6. On one island they conquered Ismarus, chief city of the Cicones; but while they feasted in celebration, _____*pandemonium*_____ broke loose.

7. The Cicones had returned with reinforcements; the Greeks _____*succumbed*_____ to the force of this great army.

8. Another episode occurred in the land of the one-eyed giants, where the Greeks found it _____*crucial*_____ to outwit Polyphemus, the chief of the Cyclopes, in order to escape from the island.

9. They did escape, but as they fled from shore in their ships, the furious giant _____*catapulted*_____ a huge rock into the sea, narrowly missing them.

Review 8

These sentences are based on world history. Write the letter of the item that could correctly substitute for the italicized portion, giving the same meaning.

__c__ 1. Martin Luther led the Reformation in Germany, stressing Scripture as the Christian's sole authority and faith as the only basis of salvation. Meanwhile, *his contemporaries* in other European countries were making the same emphases.
  a. Roman Catholic leaders
  b. his rivals
  c. men living at the same time

__b__ 2. Before the Reformation, superstitious fears were common; the strong preaching of the reformers *dispelled* many of those fears.
  a. built up
  b. drove out
  c. clarified

__a__ 3. Many came to realize how *preposterous* was the teaching that indulgences could provide pardon for sins.
  a. absurd
  b. dangerous
  c. helpful

__b__ 4. When Luther returned from a journey to Rome, he *portrayed* that city as it was, a place where even church leaders indulged in sin of every kind.
  a. understood
  b. described
  c. condemned

__c__ 5. Church leaders arranged a debate between Luther and a well-known scholar; they no doubt thought there was no *appreciable* difference between Luther and other monks.
  a. great
  b. understandable
  c. noticeable

__a__ 6. The pope used the Inquisition against the Protestant movement. Those accused of *heresy* were assumed to be guilty until proved innocent, and torture was a frequent means of obtaining a confession.
  a. false doctrine
  b. disobedience
  c. giving their inheritances to Luther

__c__ 7. Luther and other reformers translated Scripture into the spoken languages, such as German and English. Reading the Bible and hearing it faithfully preached enabled people to *discriminate* between truth and error.
  a. shift
  b. debate
  c. differentiate

With these combining forms make ten English words, adding endings if necessary.

anti-/ant-	para-/par-	chrono/chron	onym	thes/thet
epi-/ep-	peri-	graph	phras	
hyper-	syn-/sym-	meter/metr	therm	

1. _____antithesis_____
2. _____hyperthermia_____
3. _____epigraph_____
4. _____perimeter_____
5. _____chronometer_____

6. _____thermometer_____
7. _____periphrasis_____
8. _____synthesis_____
9. _____symmetry_____
10. _____telegraph_____

Also antithetic, antonym, paragraph, parameter, para- phrase, periphrastic, symmetrical, syn- onym, synonymous, synthetic, etc.

The following sentences are based mainly on a first-hand account of the settling of the area of Otsego, New York, beginning in 1785. William Cooper, father of James Fenimore Cooper, bought many foreclosed mortgages and then sold forty thousand acres to settlers.

Choose from these words to complete the sentences, using the past tense of verbs if necessary.

agnostic	atheist	domesticated	enthusiasm	obliterate
anonymous	caustic	empathy	inference	panacea

1. Although William Cooper had more money than those who bought his land, he had an _____empathy_____ for their hardships; he also was making a home in the wilderness.

2. Time and progress tend to _____obliterate_____ stories of pioneer hardships; if Cooper had not written about the adversities faced in this settlement, the settlers' story would not have been told.

3. The few settlers who owned one or two _____domesticated_____ animals had to let them "range the woods for subsistence."

4. Cooper "established potash works among the settlers"; they used potash, a _____caustic_____ substance, to fertilize their fields.

5. Like many American pioneers, Cooper speaks of "a good Providence." Unlike _____atheists_____ , who deny the existence of God, he recognized that God provided for the settlers in a time of great need.

6. Although Cooper does not state his motive for starting the settlement at Otsego, the reader's _____inference_____ is that he was a kind man, wanting to help these who were of the "poorest order of men."

7. In a surprisingly short time, the _____enthusiasm_____ and hard work of Cooper and the other settlers changed this part of the wilderness to a place of farms, "schools, academies, churches, meeting-houses, turnpike roads, and a market town."

Review 10

Complete each statement, basing your answer on the meaning of the italicized word.

1. A *philosopher* loves ___wisdom___ .

2. A *bibliophile* loves ___books___ .

3. The *prologue* comes at the ___beginning___ of a book or play.

4. The *epilogue* comes at the ___end___ of a book or play.

5. A *synthesis* involves putting parts ___together___ .

6. A person who is *dogmatic* speaks positively about principles that ___cannot___ be proved.

7. In a *cryptic* message the information is ___hidden/secret___ .

8. An *orthodox* book is, according to an accepted standard, ___right___ teaching.

9. A *heterodox* book, according to an accepted standard, contains ___unacceptable/wrong___ teaching.

10. A *logical* statement is ___reasonable___ .

11. In Hebrews 12 we see the Christian life as *analogous* to running a race; in other words, it is ___similar to___ running a race.

12. No honest person would advertise a *panacea,* for no medicine can cure ___all___ diseases.

13. A person suffering from *hypothermia* has probably been in a very ___cold___ place.

14. An *anonymous* letter is usually discarded, because the writer has not supported his statements with his ___name___ .

Review 11

In the space provided, write the word selected from the list that can logically precede the item in the second column.

abysmal   consecutive   era   metric
anemic   embers   indomitable   varsity
canter   enumerate   maternal

1. ___maternal___ grandmother

2. ___indomitable___ force of the army

3. ___consecutive___ days

4. ___abysmal___ depths

5. ___anemic___ condition caused by poor nutrition

6. _____metric_____ decimal system of measurement

7. _____varsity_____ basketball team

8. _____era_____ of progress

9. _____embers_____ of the campfire

10. _____enumerate_____ his successes

11. _____canter_____ to the stable

Review 12

Select from these words to complete the sentences, changing the verb form if necessary.

abyss	confirm	impending
assert	distinctive	invincible
capricious	distort	pensive
compile	drawing room	whimsical
comprise		

1. A _____distinctive_____ quality of *Pilgrim's Progress* is the spiritual help it has been to Christians for three centuries.

2. This perennially popular book by John Bunyan _____comprises_____ an allegorical narration of typical problems and temptations faced by Christians.

3. Rather than _____assert_____ great Bible truths, as in a sermon, the author dramatizes these truths.

4. As the story begins, Christian (the main character) is weeping and trembling because of _____impending_____ judgment that he is reading about in the Book.

5. Christian's distress over the spiritual need of his relatives _____confirms_____ in their minds that he needs a physical cure for this distress.

6. When Evangelist talks with him, Christian expresses fear of falling into Tophet, apparently referring to the _____abyss_____ of hell.

7. At the cross, Christian is set free from his burden of sin; but his salvation does not make him _____invincible_____ when he faces temptations.

8. Mr. Worldly Wiseman _____compiles_____ for Christian a list of troubles and dangers that lie ahead for him.

9. This "Wiseman" then _____distorts_____ the truth about God's law, telling Christian that by following this law he can get rid of his sin.

10. Then Christian comes to Interpreter's house and enters the _____drawing room_____ , or parlor, where he learns that Christ, not the law, cleanses sin from the heart.

11. Bunyan wrote *Pilgrim's Progress* as though he had seen it in a dream. However, it is not _____whimsical_____ , as are many fanciful "dream" stories.

40

Review 13

Write the letter for the word that matches the definition.

_c_ 1. weakly sentimental; indecisive, spineless
  a. hoity-toity
  b. hugger-mugger
  c. namby-pamby
  d. higgledy-piggledy

_a_ 2. be on friendly terms; associate familiarly
  a. hobnob
  b. mishmash
  c. tittle-tattle
  d. flimflam

_d_ 3. insincere, empty talk
  a. flip-flop
  b. hobnob
  c. flimflam
  d. claptrap

_b_ 4. affectedly refined, mincing
  a. wishy-washy
  b. niminy-piminy
  c. helter-skelter
  d. willy-nilly

_b_ 5. an antiaircraft gun
  a. hubbub
  b. ack-ack
  c. humdrum
  d. fiddle-faddle

_d_ 6. bewildering excitement
  a. flimflam
  b. claptrap
  c. tittle-tattle
  d. razzle-dazzle

_c_ 7. waste time in indecision or hesitation
  a. helter-skelter
  b. chitchat
  c. shilly-shally
  d. higgledy-piggledy

_a_ 8. mixture of unrelated things
  a. mishmash
  b. riffraff
  c. harum-scarum
  d. ragtag

To entertain children and educate them about England's early history, Rudyard Kipling wrote a series of stories called *Puck of Pook's Hill.* The following sentences are based on the first of these stories, "Weland's Sword." If you've never read these stories, you would find them an enjoyable way to learn a bit of history.

Use these words to complete the sentences.

affable	dejected	droll	pensively	quench

1. While Dan and Una were amusing themselves by acting out parts of Shakespeare's *Midsummer Night's Dream,* a _____*droll*_____ little creature appeared on their "stage."

2. Although he looked strange—"a small, brown, broad-shouldered, pointy-eared person"—he was easy to talk to; and soon the children were talking freely with their _____*affable*_____ new friend, Puck.

3. He began to tell them about the ancient invaders of England, especially the Danes, and their god Weland. Dan and Una listened _____*pensively*_____ as their little visitor told them about the cruelty of Weland.

4. Only sacrifices of horses and of men could _____*quench*_____ the desire of Weland for human worship.

5. According to Puck's story, people gradually quit making these sacrifices, and Weland had to work, thanklessly, as a blacksmith. He became _____*dejected*_____ because no one appreciated him or his work.

41

Follow the same directions for each set of words: before each phrase write the word from the list that can logically begin that phrase.

capricious	embellished	omnibus	sumptuous	wayward
congenial	impediment	precarious	vantage	

1. _____precarious_____ position at the edge of the canyon

2. _____omnibus_____ of mystery stories

3. _____vantage_____ point at the top of the Empire State Building

4. _____capricious_____ actions with no evident motive or plan

5. _____wayward_____ son who caused sorrow to his parents

6. _____embellished_____ with ornate decorations

7. _____impediment_____ to progress

8. _____congenial_____ friends with a good sense of humor

9. _____sumptuous_____ meal served Thanksgiving evening

commence	temerity	vigilant
prodigious	turbulent	vulnerable

1. _____vulnerable_____ position of the warship in the enemy's territory

2. _____turbulent_____ crowd, refusing to disperse

3. _____commence_____ the speech by telling an anecdote

4. _____vigilant_____ through the night because of the threat of danger

5. _____temerity_____ of the hunter where grizzly bears had been sighted

6. _____prodigious_____ size of the whale, when compared to its relative the dolphin

Write the letter for the item that correctly completes the statement in accordance with the meaning of the italicized word.

__b__ 1. What is the effect of an *anesthetic?*
   a. increased energy
   b. lack of feeling
   c. better understanding

__c__ 2. What kind of phrase is a *cliché?*
   a. one that has just been discovered
   b. one that is misunderstood
   c. one that is overused

__c__ 3. What does a *commendable* act deserve?
   a. criticism
   b. analysis
   c. praise

__a__ 4. If a report that we are preparing contains *discrepancies,* what should we do before presenting it?
   a. correct any factual errors
   b. check the punctuation
   c. be sure the opening and closing are effective

_c_ 5. When a composer writes _fortissimo_ before a section in a piece of music, how does he want it to be played or sung?

    a. very softly
    b. very fast
    c. very loudly

_a_ 6. How does a _frugal_ person spend money?

    a. without wasting any
    b. by check
    c. only at the end of the month

_c_ 7. How does a doctor treat _hyperthermia?_

    a. by taking the patient's temperature
    b. by the standard treatment for frostbite
    c. by lowering the patient's temperature

_b_ 8. How would you describe a person who owns _megabucks?_

    a. intelligent
    b. rich
    c. in debt

_c_ 9. What is a _microbe?_

    a. a small garment
    b. a large map
    c. a tiny disease-causing life form

_a_ 10. What is a _morsel?_

    a. a small bite of something
    b. more of something
    c. a word with a superlative suffix

_c_ 11. What does the term _peccadillo_ mean?

    a. an Australian animal
    b. a tiny pencil
    c. a small sin or fault

_b_ 12. What does the instruction _pianissimo_ mean?

    a. play on a very small piano
    b. that a person should play or sing very softly or quietly
    c. that the music should be very slow

_b_ 13. Why would you make a _preferable choice?_

    a. It is easily understood.
    b. It is more desirable than another.
    c. It needs an immediate answer.

Supplement

Keep Building (Lessons 1, 3–4, 6–7, 9–10)

Now that you have worked with several Greek combining forms, you could add to these year after year. You might begin a notebook, or a section in your loose-leaf notebook, where you add more of these as you discover them. Leave space for words made from these combining forms and write them in as you come across them. A standard dictionary includes prefixes and suffixes, with their meanings, in the regular word listing. Also, if a word contains a prefix and a root, the etymology section of the word entry gives the meaning of each part.

You might begin your list with these, which are complete Greek words.

biblion, "book"	hudor (hydr) "water"	phos/photos, "light"
bios, "life"	lithos, "stone"	physis, "nature"
cardia (kardia), "heart"	morphe, "shape"	pneuma, "wind, breath"
ge, "earth"	osteon, "bone"	polis, "city"
glossa, "tongue"	petros, "rock"	pur (pyr), "fire"

Same Letters, Different Words (1–5, 6–10, 11–15)

Rearrange the letters of the word(s) in the first column to make the word for the second column. For some of the words you will need to add or subtract a letter or two, as shown in the example. The lesson number for the word is indicated in parentheses. An asterisk (*) before the word indicates that it is found in a Challenger or Word Story.

The challenge will be greater if you first try all the words without looking at the lessons in which they are explained.

This could be a contest, and you could follow the contest rules on page 51.

Lessons 1–5

Example

treat + c, l ___*clatter*___ (2) = make a rattling sound

1. retain − a ___*inert*___ (2) = unable to move

2. wore + s, b ___*browse*___ (2) = graze; read casually

3. day + rim ___*myriad*___ (2) = vast number

4. plug ___*gulp*___ (2) = swallow greedily

5. real + b ___*blare*___ (2) = sound loudly and insistently

6. dart + he ___*dearth*___ (4) = scarcity; famine

7. tap + hay *___*apathy*___ (4) = lack of feeling

8. hop + sat ___*pathos*___ (4) = quality that causes sympathy

9. alum + q ___*qualm*___ (5) = feeling of doubt

10. not a cliff + i ___*affliction*___ (4) = pain and suffering

Lessons 6–10

1. never + f, t   _fervent_   (6) = intense

2. undated   _daunted_   (6) = dismayed

3. path + neon   _pantheon_   (7) = temple for all gods

4. fence + rein   _inference_   (8) = conclusion from evidence

5. yes + her   _heresy_   (8) = false doctrine

6. mince + a   _anemic_   (9) = weak and pale

7. these antics   _anesthetics_   (9) = substances that cause loss of feeling

8. on + so + many + u   _anonymous_   (9) = having unacknowledged authorship

9. this tea   _atheist_   (9) = one who denies the existence of God

10. pay them   _empathy_   (9) = feeling what another person feels

11. atomic + d, g   _dogmatic_   (10) = stating something in an authoritative or arrogant manner

12. loop + argue − a   _prologue_   (10) = lines introducing a literary work

13. tears   _aster_   (10) = a star-shaped flower

Lessons 11–15

1. nail + cone + g   _congenial_   (11) = harmonious, pleasant

2. in + cute + coves   _consecutive_   (11) = coming one after another

3. mere + tune + a   _enumerate_   (11) = to name one by one

4. crate + n   _canter_   (11) = pace of a horse

5. domain + bite + l   _indomitable_   (11) = unconquerable

6. tears + s   _assert_   (12) = to state positively

7. merit + yet   _temerity_   (14) = bold and rash disregard of danger

8. time + dime + p, n   _impediment_   (14) = hindrance, obstruction

9. lag + fur   _frugal_   (15) = not wasteful

10. leave + blur + n   _vulnerable_   (14) = able to be wounded

Twenty Questions (Lessons 1–8)

The class is divided into two teams, each of which hopes to answer ten questions correctly. (If a team has more than ten members, some may pair up to answer their questions together.) The first five questions below are directed to Team A. For each correct answer, based on the meaning of the italicized word(s), the team receives a point. If the answer is incorrect, the right answer is, of course, the other choice. The second five questions go to Team B, and so on.

1. Is a short poem on a single thought an *epigram* or an *epigraph?* *epigram*

2. If something is *accessible,* is it easy or difficult to obtain? *easy*

3. If something is *receding,* is it moving toward you or away from you? *away from you*

4. Which is *inert,* a dead elephant or an elephant running through the forest? *a dead one*

5. When are weeds *prolific,* during a drought or during a rainy season? *during a rainy season*

6. If there is a *rift* in a friendship, have the friends been reunited or has a disagreement separated them? *A disagreement has separated them.*

7. Is a person who is living a *bucolic* life *rustic* or *domesticated?* *rustic*

8. Does the frequent use of *periphrasis* make a person's writing less clear or more clear to the reader? *less clear*

9. Are the boundaries of a ball field called its *parameter* or its *perimeter?* *perimeter*

10. Would the judges of a contest first establish *criteria* or *equilibrium* as a basis for judging? *criteria*

11. Which is not provable by any existing standards, *telepathy* or *symmetry?* *telepathy*

12. If a speaker praises someone, does he *exhort* or *extol* that person? *he extols*

13. Does the root of *epidemic* mean "people" or "name"? *people*

14. Is a *polygraph* used to determine how many books a certain person has written or whether he tells the truth? *whether he tells the truth*

15. Is a *furtive* look a sly look or a bold look? *a sly look*

16. Which is a *perennial* problem, one that must be faced year after year, or one permanently solved in a single meeting? *one that must be faced year after year*

17. Is *filial* love the love of a child for his parents or of a man for his wife? *love of a child for his parents*

18. If there is a *dearth* of information about a certain topic, would writing a thorough report on that topic be easy or difficult? *difficult*

19. If there is *dissension* in a home, do the family members get along well together or quarrel? *quarrel*

20. If a person *spurns* your offer to help him, does he reject or accept your help? *rejects it*

Twenty Questions (Lessons 9–15)

The class is divided into two teams, each of which hopes to answer ten or more questions correctly based on vocabulary words. (If a team has more than ten members, some can pair up to answer their questions together.) This can be an open-book contest if the teacher wishes. The first five questions below are directed first to Team A. Each answer (a word, a phrase, or a sentence) involves the meaning of a word found in Lessons 9-15. If a team member (or pair) cannot answer the question, or answers incorrectly, the question goes to a member (or pair) on the other team. If neither team answers correctly, the teacher will give the answer. The second five questions go first to Team B, and so on. For each correct answer, a team receives one point.

1. What is the meaning of the prefix in *anemia, atheist, anonymous,* and *abyss? not, without*

2. What is the meaning of the root in *atheist* and *enthusiasm? a god*

3. What is the meaning of the root found in all three of these words: *pseudonym, anonymous,* and *synonym? name*

4. What is the meaning of the combining form shared by the words *dogmatic, orthodox,* and *heterodox? opinion; teaching*

5. What is the meaning of the combining form shared by the words *philosopher, Philadelphia,* and *bibliophile? love*

6. What are two words from the Greek word meaning "star"? *aster, asterisk*

7. What is the original word from which each of these words was clipped: *canter, varsity,* and *bunk? Canterbury, university, Buncombe (County)*

8. If a person is *indomitable,* what does he not do? *give in*

9. If all family members are *congenial,* what do they not do? *quarrel*

10. If you *compile* information, what do you do with it? *gather it from several sources into one place*

11. If a person does not *distort* the facts, what does he avoid doing? *misrepresenting or twisting the facts*

12. If a student's report is a *mishmash,* what fault does it have? *It is a mixture of unrelated statements.*

13. You should beware of people engaged in *flimflam.* What harm could they do to you? *cheat, swindle, or deceive you*

14. Why would you enjoy being with an *affable* person? *He would be friendly and easy to talk with.*

15. What kind of danger is involved in a *precarious* situation? *lack of security or stability*

16. In I Peter 5:8, we are told that because of the Devil's ways we are to be *vigilant.* What should we do to obey this command? *be alert, watchful*

17. What does a *frugal* person avoid? *wastefulness*

18. If the testimony of a witness in a courtroom contains *discrepancies,* what will the opposing attorney undoubtedly point out to the jury? *that the statements are inconsistent*

19. Why should we avoid the frequent use of *clichés? They lack freshness./They have been overused.*

20. Why would a military leader encourage bravery but discourage *temerity? Temerity is boldness with a foolish disregard for danger.*

Word Puzzles (Lessons 1–8, 9–15)

Lessons 1–8
List below all the vocabulary words you find.
recedepidemiconcedearthazardouscamperenniallayoffilial

1. _____recede_____   6. _____scamper_____

2. _____epidemic_____   7. _____perennial_____

3. _____concede_____   8. _____allay_____

4. _____dearth_____   9. _____layoff_____

5. _____hazardous_____   10. _____filial_____

Lessons 9–15
List below all the vocabulary words you find.
disasterabyssumptuousubmarinemberagtagnostichitchatheist

1. _____disaster_____   6. _____ember_____

2. _____era_____   7. _____ragtag_____

3. _____abyss_____   8. _____agnostic_____

4. _____sumptuous_____   9. _____chitchat_____

5. _____submarine_____   10. _____atheist_____

Crossword Puzzle (Lessons 1–15)

In this puzzle you will find two words from each of the fifteen lessons.

Across

2. coming one after the other without a break
4. give a false or misleading account
7. rustic; characteristic of country life
11. free from disturbance; calm
13. period of economic decline
17. about to take place; hovering threateningly
19. lover or collector of books
21. inconsistency; difference between statement and fact
24. scarcity; famine
26. prediction of probable outcome of a disease
27. concluding section of a literary work
28. lasting for several years; perpetual
29. a rewording of something

Down

1. blot out; destroy, leaving no trace

3. adorn; make fanciful by ornamental details
4. put off, take off
5. brief statement or outline of a subject
6. behaving as a disorderly crowd
8. the act of seeking
9. yield to a superior power or great desire
10. make afraid or discouraged
12. unconquerable
14. position that gives comprehensive view
15. intense; showing great emotion
16. incapable of being measured; extreme
18. drive away; scatter
20. little sin or fault
22. of greatest importance; severe
23. insincere, empty talk
25. admit that something is true; grant as a privilege

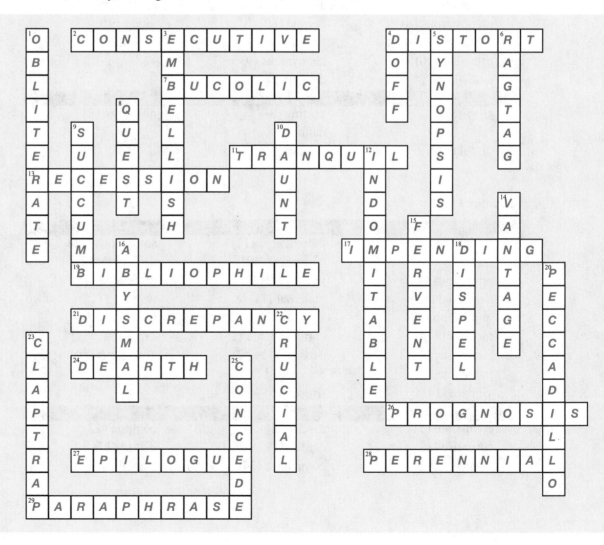

Logical Contexts (Lessons 1–5, 6–10, 11–15)

This could be a whole-class project or a contest. Doing this practice orally will help increase your "feel" for the right use of the words. For each adjective, give a noun that it could logically modify; for each verb, give a noun that could logically be its direct object. Mark any words that no one in the class answers satisfactorily, and include such words in future practices.

Lessons 1–5

Adjectives		
accessible (1)	domesticated (2)	compatible (3)
prolific (2)	tranquil (2)	metric (4)
filial (3)	perennial (3)	
pathetic (4)	inert (2)	

Verbs		
concede (1)	don (5)	extol (4)
gulp (2)	spurn (5)	doff (5)
delude (5)	telegraph (1)	exhort (5)

Lessons 6–10

Adjectives		
fervent (6)	abysmal (9)	caustic (8)
preposterous (8)	cryptic (10)	giddy (9)
analogous (10)	hazardous (7)	logical (10)
orthodox (10)	anonymous (9)	
crucial (7)	dogmatic (10)	

Verbs		
allay (6)	portray (8)	obliterate (8)
relish (6)	daunt (6)	
dispel (8)	catapult (7)	

Lessons 11–15

Adjectives		
acute (11)	indomitable (11)	sumptuous (11)
distinctive (12)	whimsical (12)	droll (13)
prodigious (14)	vulnerable (14)	preferable (15)
congenial (11)	maternal (11)	wayward (11)
impending (12)	affable (13)	humdrum (13)
turbulent (14)	commendable (15)	capricious (12)
consecutive (11)	pensive (11)	precarious (14)
invincible (12)	dejected (13)	
vigilant (14)	frugal (15)	

Verbs		
enumerate (11)	assert (12)	compile (12)
comprise (12)	confirm (12)	distort (12)
quench(13)	commence (14)	embellish (14)

Ticktacktoe   (Lessons 1–5, 6–10, 11–15)

The class is divided into two teams. Each team chooses a representative, and these two compete for one or two games. Then each of these selects another to replace him, and so on.

The rules are simple. The teacher will announce whether this is an open- or closed-book contest. The contestant is to give the word that is defined. If the word is correct, he may put his *X* or *O* where he chooses. If the answer is incorrect, the other team receives the same question. If neither team answers correctly, the teacher will give the answer. As soon as either team or contestant completes a vertical, horizontal, or diagonal line, a point is awarded and a new ticktacktoe is begun.

Lessons 1–5

1. a short poem written on a single thought *epigram*

2. able to be reached easily *accessible*

3. the sound made when a person uses a file on wood or metal *rasp*

4. the sound of noisy swallowing *gulp*

5. tame; adapted to life associated with man *domesticated*

6. graze; read casually, skim *browse*

7. producing in great abundance *prolific*

8. the wordy, roundabout way of saying something *periphrasis*

9. the length of a boundary around an area *perimeter*

10. a standard or basis for judging *criterion*

11. not existing in living form now *extinct*

12. pain and suffering *affliction*

13. strife and discord *dissension*

14. results of a misfortune or disaster *aftermath*

15. reject disdainfully; scorn *spurn*

16. feeling of doubt; pang of conscience *qualm*

Lessons 6–10

1. exact opposite *antithesis*

2. the combining of parts to form a whole *synthesis*

3. tremble; speak in a quivering voice *quaver*

4. relieve; reduce the intensity of *allay*

5. a violent upheaval, such as a flood *cataclysm*

6. yield to a superior power *succumb*

7. cure-all, said to be a remedy for diseases or evils *panacea*

8. *adj.,* belonging to the same period of time; *noun,* one who belongs to the same period of time   *contemporary*

9. make a clear distinction; distinguish   *discriminate*

10. false or unorthodox doctrine; adherence to false doctrine   *heresy*

11. incapable of being measured; extreme   *abysmal*

12. ability to participate in another person's feelings or thoughts   *empathy*

13. a person who loves or collects books   *bibliophile*

14. authoritative or arrogant in stating something that is unproved or unprovable   *dogmatic*

15. hidden; secret; mysterious; puzzling   *cryptic*

16. study of population   *demographics*

Lessons 11–15

1. pleasant; associated together harmoniously   *congenial*

2. coming one after the other without a break   *consecutive*

3. unconquerable; not able to be put down   *indomitable*

4. lacking consistency; imaginative; fanciful   *whimsical*

5. unpredictable; apt to change suddenly   *capricious*

6. to state, often in a formal, authoritative way   *assert*

7. easy to talk with; friendly, gracious   *affable*

8. weakly sentimental; indecisive, spineless   *namby-pamby*

9. willingly or unwillingly; disorganized   *willy-nilly*

10. extinguish; suppress; put an end to, destroy   *quench*

11. enormous; extraordinary; marvelous   *prodigious*

12. position giving a comprehensive view or strategic advantage   *vantage*

13. worthy of praise   *commendable*

14. not wasteful or spending unnecessarily; inexpensive, meager   *frugal*

15. a little fault   *peccadillo*

16. difference; inconsistency; lack of agreement   *discrepancy*

Analogies (Lessons 1–15)

To complete these analogies, your class might work together or in groups of three or four. The first step is to decide what relationship the second word (or word part) has to the first. Then complete the analogy with a word (or word part) that shows the same relationship in the second half as in the first. Look for relationships such as these:

shift in part of speech
related word parts
words shortened
words blended

related meanings
opposite meanings
spelling changes

Example:

anemia : anemic :: anesthesia : _____anesthetic_____

This means that *anemia* is to *anemic* as *anesthesia* is to *anesthetic*.
(A noun is to an adjective as a noun is to an adjective.)

1. astrologer : astrology :: astronomer : _____astronomy_____

2. Buncombe : bunk :: Canterbury : _____canter_____

3. telegraph : telegram :: epigraph : _____epigram_____

4. kataclysm : cataclysm :: kriterion : _____criterion_____

5. memorandum : memo :: advertisement : _____ad_____

6. clangor : fire engine :: blare : _____trumpet_____

7. Adam : Adkins :: Peter : _____Perkins_____

8. American Indian : Amerindian :: cable television : _____cablevision_____

9. riff : raff :: flim : _____flam_____

10. mishmash : flip-flop :: chitchat : _____wishy-washy, shilly-shally, fiddle-faddle, etc._____

11. huper- : hyper- :: hupo- : _____hypo-_____

12. heterodox : orthodox :: hyperthermia : _____hypothermia_____

13. para- : alongside; near :: peri- : _____about, around_____

14. anti- : against :: syn- : _____together, with_____

15. philosopher : wisdom :: bibliophile : _____books_____

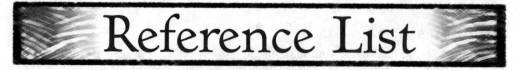

Reference List

of Word Parts in Levels A–C

Prefixes

a-/ab-/abs- "away from"
ad- "to, toward"
ante- "before, in front of"
circum- "around, about"
con-/com- "with, together"; intensifier of root meaning
contra- "against, opposite, contrasting; lower in pitch"
counter- "contrary, opposite, opposing; corresponding"
de- "down from, concerning"
dis-/di- "apart, away"
e-/ex- "out, from, out from"
extra-/extro- "outside of, beyond"
in- "in, on, within"
in- "not"
inter- "between, among"
intra- "within"
intro- "in, inward"
ob- "against, toward"
per- "through"
post- "after"
pre- "before"
pro- "for, favoring; in place of; forth, forward"
re- "again, back, backwards"
retro- "back, backwards"
se- "apart"
sub- "under"
super-/supr- "excessive, more than normal; above, over"
trans-/tra- "across"

Roots

act "do"
bene "well, good"
cede/cess "go"
cept "take"
clude/clus "close"
dic/dict "speak, say"
fact "make, do"
fer "bring, bear"
flu "flow"
grade/gress "step, go"
greg "herd, flock; company"

ject "throw, cast, or hurl"

leg/lect "read; choose"

lude/lus "play"

male "badly, bad"

mit/miss "send"

pel/pulse "drive"

pone/pose "place, put"

port "carry"

press "press"

reg/rect "right, straight"

rupt "break"

scribe/script "write"

sent/sense "feel, think"

spect "look at, watch"

terr "earth"

tract "draw, pull"

vene/vent "come"

vert/verse "turn"

vide/vise "see"

voke/voc "call"

vol "wish, want"

Suffixes

-ance/-ence/-ancy/-ency "condition or state; act"

-ant/-ent *adj.* "performing or causing a particular action; being in a particular condition"; *noun,* "one that does or causes a particular action"

-ate "act upon in a particular manner"

-ion "action, process; result of an action or process"

-ous "having, full of, possessing the qualities of"

Index

Prefixes

Combining Forms

Suffixes

Words